University of Plymouth
Charles Seale Hayne Library
Subject to status this item may be renewed
via your Voyager account

http://voyager.plymouth.ac.uk
Tel: (01752) 232323

Charles Seale-Hayne Library
University of Plymouth
(01752) 588 588
LibraryandITenquiries@plymouth.ac.uk

Symbol Grounding

Benjamins Current Topics

Special issues of established journals tend to circulate within the orbit of the subscribers of those journals. For the Benjamins Current Topics series a number of special issues have been selected containing salient topics of research with the aim to widen the readership and to give this interesting material an additional lease of life in book format.

Volume 21

Symbol Grounding
Edited by Tony Belpaeme, Stephen J. Cowley and Karl F. MacDorman

These materials were previously published in *Interaction Studies* 8:1 (2007), under de guidance of Editor-in-Chief James R. Hurford.

Symbol Grounding

Edited by

Tony Belpaeme
University of Plymouth

Stephen J. Cowley
University of Hertfordshire

Karl F. MacDorman
Indiana University

John Benjamins Publishing Company
Amsterdam / Philadelphia

™ The paper used in this publication meets the minimum requirements of American National Standard for Information Sciences – Permanence of Paper for Printed Library Materials, ANSI z39.48-1984.

Library of Congress Cataloging-in-Publication Data

Symbol grounding / edited by Tony Belpaeme, Stephen J. Cowley and Karl F. MacDorman.
    p. cm. (Benjamins Current Topics, ISSN 1874-0081 ; v. 21)
Includes bibliographical references and index.
1. Symbol grounding. 2. Artificial intelligence. I. Belpaeme, Tony. II. Cowley, Stephen J.
    (Stephen John), 1955- III. MacDorman, Karl F.
P98.5.S96S96   2009
302.2'22--dc22   2009039746
ISBN 978 90 272 2251 0   (Hb ; alk. paper)
ISBN 978 90 272 8874 5   (Eb)

John Benjamins Publishing Co. · P.O. Box 36224 · 1020 ME Amsterdam · The Netherlands
John Benjamins North America · P.O. Box 27519 · Philadelphia PA 19118-0519 · USA

Table of contents

Extending symbol grounding

Tony Belpaeme and Stephen J. Cowley
Faculty of Science and Technology, University of Plymouth /
School of Psychology, University of Hertfordshire

The contributions collected in this volume emerged from an international work-shop on symbol grounding organised at the University of Plymouth in 2006. The goal was to extend the classical view of symbol grounding by recognising that language and cognitive dynamics are mutually constitutive. Specifically, we aimed to do so by bringing researchers who study human signalling together with others who focus on simulating intelligence and language. The objectives of the work-shop were to view language and cognition as linking what goes on in the head with causal processes that are intersubjective, multimodal, affect-laden, and organised by historically rooted customs and artefacts. In this, we focus on how symbol grounding can be reconsidered when language is viewed as a dynamical process rooted in both culture and biology. This welcomes a cross-disciplinary approach and this volume contains research related to robotic or computer modelling of symbol grounding, psychological and linguistic viewpoints on cognitive development and semiotic dynamics.

By invoking symbol grounding, Harnad (1990) recognised that any computational model of mind must explain how an agent's representations (or symbols) connect with the external world (cf. Taddeo & Floridi, 2005). While Harnad used 'symbol' to denote both the agent's representations and linguistic signals, today this systematic ambiguity is widely rejected. Most agree that explaining the evolution and emergence of linguistic signals is quite unlike grounding symbols into objects beyond the skin. To understand this shift in perspective, one has to re-visit the historical context of symbol grounding. Harnad (1990) formulated the symbol grounding problem in response to Searle's (1980) famous (or notorious) *Minds, Brains, and Programs* article. In this, readers are invited to imagine a Chinese Room where a person applies rules to input and generates output. The input consists of written Chinese characters, but to that person these are senseless squiggles. As is the case for a computer program, this gives rise to output that makes sense *outside* the room, but not to the person or mechanism in the room. For many this suggests that computers cannot attain human-like intelligence. Like a parable, the text is cleverly constructed. Playing the devil's advocate, Searle first entertains the view that, because a brain is like a computer executing a program, a computer could pass the Turing Test. Second, he assumes that syntactic processing is automatic: symbols manipulated during processing make no use of meaning. By implication, any device that passes the test is of merely technical interest. Without *intentionality*, Searle insinuates, no computer can ever attach meaning to its inner symbols.[1] This is highly controversial. Harnad (1990, 2003) reinterprets it as the challenge of showing how symbols (linguistic or otherwise) *can* be connected to the world beyond the body. Without a person to interpret them, squiggles on paper or spoken words indeed lack meaning or, for Harnad, are ungrounded. Once inwardly represented, however, they connect with referent-indexed symbols and, in so doing, are *grounded*. The challenge is to show how agents can causally connect symbols to the external world. First, they need senses to identify referents which, eventually, can connect with squiggles or spoken words. To add meaning to the resulting symbols, they need sensorimotor interaction with the world. To solve the problem of symbol grounding, a machine must be a robot rather than a computer.

What kinds of *symbol* do robots need? For Harnad (1990) and computational theorists (Newell & Simon, 1976; Newell, 1980; Pylyshyn, 1984; Fodor, 1987), this is a matter of definition. Symbols are arbitrary physical tokens or syntactic combinations of such tokens that can be manipulated systematically and generatively and assigned a meaning. An agent's symbols, therefore, stand in for both physical properties (e.g., what is common to cups) and repeatable linguistic signals (e.g., spoken words). By implication, grounding symbols in cups is broadly similar to grounding them in the speech stream.

While each author in this volume accepts the classical view that (inner) symbols must connect with objects and linguistic signals, at the same time they reject the conflation of language and representation into a symbol. Generally, they propose two ways of extending the classical view of symbol grounding. First, those who take a pragmatic view draw on insights from implementing symbol grounding in simulation or on real-world robots. This leads them, first, to reject appeal to already-combined forms. Instead, symbols are viewed as arising from connections between a referent, its sensorimotor interpretation and, in some cases, a communicative signal. This is a *semiotic* interpretation of symbol (Maturana and Varela, 1992; Clancey, 1997; Clowes, 2007; Vogt, 2002, 2007). For the pragmatists, a symbol is ultimately a set of relations which connect a meaning, signal and referent. As in Peirce's semiotic model, this is constituted by a triad of interpretant, representamen and object. Symbols thus unite a system's sensorimotor capacities with its interpretative ones. To distinguish this from seeing the symbols as meaningless tokens, it has been called the *physical* symbol grounding problem (see for example Vogt, 2002). This view is increasingly being supported in several disciplines, from psycholinguistics to robotics (for an overview see de Vega, Glenberg and Graesser, 2008).

Alongside this, a second culturalist group also rejects formal definitions of symbols. They object to the view that brains use similar forms of symbols to index both objects and patterns in the speech stream. Underplaying cultural practices, the classical view exaggerates the importance of notations. By assuming that verbal patterns are grounded in notational ways, the classical approach forgets that words are ultimately physical signals that contribute to social activity. For the brain, indeed, spoken words may entirely lack symbolic representation. In **Viger** (pp. 127–144), therefore, a capacity to identify referents is the outcome of a process of acquisition. For **Worgan and Damper** (pp. 9–32), the classical approach must be extended by appeal to *signal grounding*. Finally, for **Cowley** (pp. 85–106), categorisation of spoken words is marginal during the early stages of learning to talk. The infant-caregiver dyad focuses, not on forms or referents, but on strategic modes of action that are likely to meet their conflicting needs. To simulate extended symbol grounding, therefore, robots too will need (inner) symbols with richer content than is posited in the classical model.

Language thus ceases to be a system of formal symbols. Rather, it is viewed as an external cognitive resource that allows us to acquire categories and concepts. It functions as agents coordinate behaviour and, in so doing, gain some grasp of how others perceive the world. During the process of grounding symbols in language, therefore, agents play social games that always involve (at least) two brains, human or robotic, or some combination of these systems (cf. Seabra Lopes & Chauhan, 2007). In coordinating, of course, they typically interpret each signal in different ways. Because of individual differences and the dynamic nature of cognition, neither flesh nor silicon will concur on signal meaning. Although this poses no major problems for an individual agent, it ensures that cooperation or communication must take on strategic functions. Since referents are not guaranteed, cultural processes must stabilise interaction. We use language to coordinate what we do and thereby coordinate with what signals represent (Steels and Belpaeme, 2005).

Language thus influences symbol grounding in several ways. It facilitates the acquisition of meaning: an individual no longer needs to go through a long process of exploration to acquire knowledge; it can use language to tap into knowledge present in others (Cangelosi and Harnad, 2001). Language also serves to coordinate referents between individuals: if knowledge is acquired through sensorimotor experience, language serves to align that knowledge between individuals, facilitating communication (Steels and Belpaeme, 2005). Far from being a monolithic system of determinate forms, language is a dynamic process that is shaped and propagated by users who exploit social and physical constraints. Given that language also influences symbol grounding, the symbol grounding process too must be dynamic. Further, while important in human cognition, our cognitive states (or symbols) depend on much more than verbal patterns. In extending classical views of symbol grounding, therefore, we emphasise emotion and, equally, how categories sensitise to culturally based customs and artefacts. Human interaction and, thus, human symbols, depend on more than a syntactic analysis of words. Beyond this, however, each chapter points in a different direction. First, breaking with Fodor, **Viger** argues that the emergence of reference be seen as the culmination of a learning process. Taking the opposite tack, **Cowley** (pp. 85–106) focuses on infancy to stress that the early stages of learning to talk are more dependent on affective and multimodal processes than spoken words. In an attempt to construct a general framework, **Clowes** (pp. 107–126) suggests that language is gradually internalised. Reporting ambitious work, **Vogt and Divina** (pp. 33–54) describe a model that aims at simulating the cultural processes. In building robots that learn words **Seabra Lopes and Chauhan** fall in line in finding that teaching — not categorisation — is a simpler basis for language. Finally, focusing on the evolution of phonetic forms, **Worgan and Damper** stress that many properties of human languages are likely to depend on constraints based in how articulation and audition favour learning. Such processes, of course, use the physics of speech and, thus, underpin symbol grounding.

The six chapters extend traditional views of symbol grounding in both applied and theoretical ways. At the engineering end, Worgan and Damper criticise the lack of attention paid to the physical aspects of the symbol that is grounded. Pursuing this, they present a computational model in which a shared speech code emerges between agents, and show how constraints on production, perception and acoustics influence speech signals. While Worgan and Damper are concerned with physical signals, Vogt and Divina focus on simulations of their semantic counterparts. In their paper, they present a large scale simulation in which agents socially transmit and acquire behavioural skills. As the agents communicate, their signals can have ecological relevance only if they are grounded. Vogt and Divina present the technical challenges involved and put forward a number of learning methods, such as cross-situational learning, inspired by psycholinguistic observations. The contribution of Seabra Lopes and Chauhan takes the study of symbol grounding into the real world by presenting an experiment in which an adaptive learning system acquires the meaning of objects through linguistic instruction. Besides demonstrating the characteristics of their learning method, their pragmatic approach clearly shows that implementing symbol grounding in a real-world system is a formidable challenge in which many issues – such as perception, concept representation and concept learning – remain far from solved. Cowley argues that too much attention is spent on language as the facilitating medium for symbol grounding, and he observes that infants, from an early age, bootstrap signal grounding by relying on what agents *do together*. The infant uses affect-laden interactions to acquire culturally evolved patterns that enable it to participate in a grounding process. Clowes starts out by contrasting the view of symbols as formal tokens with the view that they emerge from a semiotic agreement. In his model, he seeks to reconcile strengths of these approaches. In so doing, he starts from Vygotsky's views on language internalisation and sets out a model of symbol internalisation. In Clowes's model this process is dynamic and self-regulatory. In the most theoretical paper, therefore, Viger takes a philosophical perspective on symbol grounding. He focuses on how abstract symbols, for example, *unicorn*, can become intrinsic to thinking. While concurring with Fodor that we need a language of thought, he challenges tradition by suggesting that referents emerge from a long acquisition process. Finally, we leave the last word to MacDorman who, looking back over the workshop, proposes that we abandon the symbol system metaphor to ask how humans – and perhaps robot bodies – can construct themselves into persons (MacDorman, 2007).

The symbol grounding problem has shown more life in it than Searle's thought experiment. Indeed, our papers strongly imply that the Chinese Room parable fails because of a simplistic assumption that, as in programs, spoken words can be formally represented. In fact, as all contributors stress, semiosis involves more than form-based computation. Even though symbol grounding has been expanded over the years, by scholars collected here and elsewhere, a number of open problems remain. One of these is the role of covariation on the acquisition of meaning: the meaning of a word or utterance can often be gleaned from that of others occurring in the same context (for example using Landauer & Dumais, 1997's Latent Semantic Analysis approach). As such, not every word or linguistic construction needs grounding. But what balance is required between grounded concepts and indirectly grounded concepts? This leads us to abstract concepts, such as *truth* or *democracy*, which cannot be directly grounded, but which do have meaning. Opinions on how abstract concepts acquire meaning abound, some positing that abstract concepts are grounded as good as directly in sensorimotor experience, such as *democracy* being grounded in the experience of going voting (Glenberg & Kaschak, 2002), some believing abstract concepts to be grounded through a long series of links to grounded, perceptual concepts. These at the moment are just theories and as such are in need empirical support or, perhaps more feasibly, in need of implementation and exploration on a robotic platform. Finally, the new directions in symbol grounding thinking hinted at in introduction and further in this volume – distributed symbol grounding, signal grounding, emotion – warrant further exploration. In the book we show how new methods, such as computer simulations and robotics, and the increased collaboration between fields as disparate as philosophy and computer science sparks debate. Who knows, perhaps all this results in a new theory of symbol grounding: extended symbol grounding.

Note

1. While computational syntax makes no use of meaning, human language may differ. Accordingly, we face philosophical sticking points. Whereas Searle (1980) views intentionality (and meaning) as a causal feature of the brain, Harnad (1990) operationalises 'aboutness' in terms of how meaning can be made intrinsic to the system itself. Others trace meaning to, for example, adaptivity of living systems in an environment (di Paolo, 2005) or biosemiosis (Barbieri, 2007).

References

Barbieri, M. (2007). Is the cell a semiotic system? In: M. Barbieri (Ed.) Introduction to biosemiotics, 179-207. Springer: Berlin.

Blackmore, S. (1999). The meme machine. Oxford: Oxford University Press.

Cangelosi, A. & Harnad, S. (2001). The adaptive advantage of symbolic theft over sensorimotor toil: Grounding language in perceptual categories. *Evolution of Communication, 4*(1), 117–142.

Clowes, R. (2007). Semiotic symbols and the missing theory of thinking. *Interaction Studies,8*(1), 105–124.

Cowley, S. J. (2007). How human infants deal with symbol grounding. *Interaction Studies, 8*(1), 83–104.

De Vega, M., Glenberg, A. M., & Graesser, A. C. (Eds.). (2008). *Symbols and embodiment: Debates on meaning and cognition.* Oxford, UK: Oxford University Press.

Di Paolo, E. (2006). Autopoiesis, adaptivity teleology, agency. *Phenomenology and the Cognitive Sciences, 4 (4)* 429-452.

Fodor, J. A. (1987). Modules, frames, fridgeons, sleeping dogs and the music of the spheres. In Pylyshyn, Z. W. (Ed.) *The robot's dilemma: The frame problem in artificial intelligence* (Chapter 8). Norwood, NJ: Ablex..

Glenberg, A. M., & Kaschak, M. P. (2002). *Grounding language in action.* Psychonomic Bulletin & Review, 9(3), 558-565.

Harnad, S. (1990). The Symbol grounding problem. *Physica D, 42,* 335–346.

Harnad, S. (2003). The Symbol grounding problem. *Encyclopedia of Cognitive Sciences.* London:Macmillan/Nature.

Landauer, T. K., & Dumais, S. T. (1997). A Solution to Plato's Problem: The Latent Semantic Analysis Theory of Acquisition, Induction, and Representation of Knowledge. *Psychological Review*, 104(2), 221-240.

MacDorman, K. F. (2007). Life after the symbol system metaphor. *Interaction Studies, 8*(1), 143–158.

Newell, A. & Simon, H.A. (1976). Computer science as empirical enquiry: Symbols and search. *Communications of the ACM, 19*(3), 113–126.

Newell, A. (1980). Physical symbol systems. *Cognitive Science, 4*(4), 135–183.

Pylyshyn, Z.W. (1984). *Computation and cognition*. Cambridge, MA: The MIT Press.

Seabra Lopes, L. & Chauhan, A. (2007). How many words can my robot learn? An approach and experiments with one-class learning. *Interaction Studies, 8*(1), 53–81.

Searle, J. (1980). Minds, brains and programs. *Behavioral and Brain Sciences, 3*(3), 417–457.

Steels, L. and Belpaeme, T. (2005). Coordinating perceptually grounded categories through language. A case study for colour. *Behavioral and Brain Sciences, 24*(8), 469–529.

Taddeo, M. & Floridi, L. (2005). The symbol grounding problem: A critical review of fifteen years of research. *Journal of Experimental and Theoretical Artificial Intelligence, 17*(4), 419–445.

Viger, C. (2007). The acquired language of thought hypothesis: A theory of symbol grounding. *Interaction Studies, 8*(1), 125–142.

Vogt, P. (2002). The physical symbol grounding problem. *Cognitive Systems Research, 3*(3), 429–457.

Vogt, P. & Divina, F. (2007). Social symbol grounding and language evolution. *Interaction Studies,8*(1), 31–52.

Worgan, S. F. & Damper, R. I. (2007). Grounding symbols in the physics of speech communication. *Interaction Studies, (8)*1, 7–30.

Grounding symbols in the physics of speech communication

Simon F. Worgan and Robert I. Damper
School of Electronics and Computer Science, University of Southampton

The traditional view of symbol grounding seeks to connect an *a priori* internal representation or 'form' to its external referent. But such a 'form' is usually itself systematically composed out of more primitive parts (i.e., it is 'symbolic'), so this view ignores its grounding in the physics of the world. Some previous work simulating multiple talking/listening agents has effectively taken this stance, and shown how a shared discrete speech code (i.e., vowel system) can emerge. Taking the earlier work of Oudeyer, we have extended his model to include a dispersive force intended to account broadly for a speaker's motivation to increase auditory distinctiveness. New simulations show that vowel systems result that are more representative of the range seen in human languages. These simulations make many profound abstractions and assumptions. Relaxing these by including more physically and physiologically realistic mechanisms for talking and listening is seen as the key to replicating more complex and dynamic aspects of speech, such as consonant-vowel patterning.

Keywords: origins of speech sounds, symbol grounding, signal grounding, multi-agent simulation, self-organisation, emergent phenomena

Introduction

The computational metaphor that underpins cognitive science, much of artificial intelligence and functionalist philosophy of mind sees intelligent behaviour as the product of the workings of a formal symbol manipulation system (e.g., Newell, 1973; Minsky, 1974; Fodor, 1975; Newell and Simon, 1976; Newell, 1980, 1990; Pylyshyn, 1984; Dietrich, 1990). But this view faces a formidable problem, famously articulated by Harnad (1990) as: "How can the semantic interpretation of a formal symbol system be made *intrinsic* to the system, rather than just parasitic on the meanings in our heads?" (p. 335). Harnad calls this the *symbol grounding problem* (SGP) and comments: "The handicap has been noticed in various forms since the advent of computing" (p. 338). The earliest reference that we know is that of Mays (1951), who writes "if we grant that these machines [*i.e.,* *digital computers*] are complex pieces of symbolism,... to acquire a significance the symbols need to be linked with a set of referents" (p. 249). So if the computational metaphor is to offer any purchase in modelling and understanding cognition, the SGP poses a challenge that cannot be neglected (Cangelosi, Greco and Harnad, 2002). We take this challenge seriously, because the long-term goal of our research is to understand, via computer modelling and simulation, how speech sound categories (broadly, 'phonemes') could have emerged during language evolution, and then how these could be combined systematically to lead to utterances with semantic content.

To some the SGP is symptomatic of an incorrect view of AI and cognitive science, famously parodied as "good old-fashioned AI," or GOFAI, by Haugeland (1985). For instance, as Pfeifer and Scheirer (1999, p. 71) write, "... the symbol grounding problem is really an artifact of symbolic systems and 'disappears' if a different approach is used." The different approach they have in mind is, of course, *embodied* or *nouvelle* AI as spearheaded by Brooks (1990, 1991, 1999), which seeks to replace the central role played by symbolic representation with nonsymbolic interfacing to the physical world through cycles of perception and action, usually conceived as based on some connectionist or statistical machine learning principles. However, the complete banishment of symbolism from the scene is rather too radical for most AI scientists and cognitive psychologists, who continue to see a role for formal symbol systems, albeit in combination with some sort of connectionist component (e.g., Minsky, 1990; Harnad, 1990, 1993) in modelling and explaining the higher cognitive functions involved in, for example, using language, doing mathematics, and decision making under uncertainty, where nouvelle AI has arguably promised more than it has delivered.

Against this background, a new view of the SGP has recently arisen in which the physics of the external world plays an important and simplifying role (Sun, 2000; Vogt, 2002). Vogt (2002) coins the term *physical symbol grounding problem* and writes: "It is based on the idea that symbols should be grounded (cf. Harnad, 1990) and... they should be grounded by physical agents that interact with the world (cf. Brooks, 1990)" (p. 435). Our work is broadly consonant with this view, treating the SGP (as does Vogt, 2002) as a technical problem by way of computer simulation, although we have also been influenced in our thinking by the work of Barsalou (1999).

Quite apart from the intrinsic scientific interest in studying the emergence of human speech and language for its own sake (Damper, 2000), it makes an excellent context in which to consider the SGP. First and foremost, we believe human communication to be the clearest, certainly best-developed, example of externally-grounded cognition. As Vogt (2002, p. 431) writes, "language through its conventions offers a basis for invariant labeling of the real world." Since human communication is a social phenomenon, we pursue an approach of multi-agent simulation, not unlike much previous work in 'language games' but with one important difference (see below).

In particular in this paper, we argue that the emergence of speech sound categories can and should be grounded in the physics of speech communication between agents, recognising that the human's contact with the external world of sound is via their articulatory and auditory systems. Important previous work along these lines is that of Steels (1997, 1998, 1999, 2003), de Boer (2000, 2001, 2005), and Oudeyer (2005a, 2005b, 2005c), who have explored grounded speech-category formation by computer simulation of multi-agent systems, with agents equipped with rudimentary articulatory and auditory systems and associated 'neural' processing. Broadly speaking, this line of work had its beginnings in the early and influential efforts of Lindblom (1986) and his colleagues to explain the origins of vowel systems in the world's languages (Liljencrantz and Lindblom, 1972; Lindblom, MacNeilage and Studdert-Kennedy, 1984; Lindblom, 1986, 2000) based on "adaptive dispersion theory." In their numerical simulations, the clustering of vowels in some metric space was predicted by minimising an energy function designed to reflect perceptual distinctiveness. An important question is exactly how realistic the simulations have to be (e.g., in terms of faithfully modelling the articulatory/auditory systems and brain mechanisms). Hence, our longer-term goal is to answer this question, although at this stage we will restrict ourselves to relatively simple simulations such as have been used in previous work.

Although Steels (1997) argues for a "limited rationality constraint" in multi-agent simulations (i.e., agents should not have access to each other's internal states), this constraint is typically violated in language games where nonlinguistic feedback figures importantly. For instance, de Boer (2001) writes, "the initiator then communicates the success or failure to the imitator using nonlinguistic communication" (p. 52). In our view, this amounts to a form of 'mind-reading,' seriously undermining the credibility of the simulations. Hence, we wish to avoid this aspect of language games, and favour Oudeyer's alternative approach where he dispenses with nonlinguistic feedback. As he writes, "it is crucial to note that agents *do not* imitate each other... The only consequence of hearing a vocalization is that it increases the probability, for the agent that hears it, of vocalizations... similar to those of the heard vocalization" (Oudeyer, p. 443). In spite of the absence of structured, coordinated interactions between agents, he achieves two results in his simulations which mirror important aspects of real language: "on the one hand discreteness and compositionality arise thanks to the coupling between perception and production within agents, on the other hand shared systems of phonemic categories arise thanks to the coupling across agents" (Oudeyer, p. 445).

A related line of investigation is that of Kirby (2001) and Kirby and Hurford (2002) who describe the iterated learning model (ILM). This, however, operates at the syntactic level, that is, learning agents receive from adult agents "meaning-signal pairs" (p. 103) that act as training data. Thus, the ILM already tacitly assumes the emergence of phonetic distinctiveness. Whereas the language-game style of simulations are concerned with language change once the basic mechanisms are in place, by contrast, Oudeyer is concerned with the earliest origins of a phonemic sound system, as are we. Further, Oudeyer's model is based on horizontal cultural interaction between agents of the same generation, following the works of Steels and colleagues, whereas the ILM is based on iterated learning among agents of one generation and agents of the previous generation (so this is more vertical learning).

However, Oudeyer's work has its own drawback in that he ignores the tenets of dispersion theory. "There are no internal forces which act as a pressure to have a repertoire of different discrete sounds," he writes (p. 443). But to cite de Boer (2001, p. 61), a successful vowel system has "its vowel clusters… dispersed (for low energy) and compact (for high imitative success)." These ideas are broadly consistent with notions of H&H theory (Lindblom, 1990) and the dispersion-focalisation theory (DFT) of Schwartz et al. (1997). Although Oudeyer tries to argue that the lack of a dispersion force is a virtue of his simulations (it is one less assumption), he also seems to recognise that it causes problems for the emergence of sound systems with realistically large numbers of vowels, writing, "Functional pressure to develop efficient communication systems might be necessary here" (p. 447).

Accordingly, the principal purpose of the present paper is to introduce ideas of H&H theory and DFT into Oudeyer-style simulations in the belief that more realistic vowel systems (i.e., more representative of those seen in a variety of human languages) will result. We will do this by extending the topological spaces in the neural maps used to couple auditory and articulatory processing as a vastly-simplified form of brain. We call these extensions *contour spaces*. The work is intended to form a baseline for future work in which we will study the impact of increased realism of the agents' articulatory and auditory capabilities, as well as extending our simulations beyond prediction of static vowel systems to the emergence of connected speech sounds with appropriate consonant-vowel patterning.

The remainder of this paper is structured as follows. In the next section, we set out our conception of physical symbol grounding, which we call *signal grounding*, and relate this to more traditional views of symbol grounding. Then, as a baseline for later discussion of our own work, we briefly describe Oudeyer's simulations of the emergence of vowel systems shared between a population of agents. We then introduce our extension to these simulations in the form of contour spaces and illustrate the beneficial effects of this extension in terms of emergence of more realistic vowel systems. Finally, we discuss the implication of these findings and conclude by arguing for the use of more realistic articulatory/auditory modelling as necessary to move beyond production of static vowel systems and account for the dynamic consonant-vowel patterning of speech.

Signal and Symbol Grounding

Before proceeding, it is necessary to discuss our relatively wide view of 'symbol grounding' and how it relates to the traditional, rather-narrower symbol grounding paradigm. Traditionally, the SGP has been seen as the problem of linking an internal symbolic representation like *cat* to the external (distal) object 'cat'. For instance, Figure 1 (reproduced from the influential text of Pfeifer and Scheirer, 1999) depicts a scenario linking the symbol *cup* with its external referent 'cup'. But this traditional view already assumes the existence of some sort of internal representation, which is more or less symbolic (or at least compositional). In our view, any solution to the SGP must also explain how this internal representation gets composed from elementary parts, which we take to be close to the notion of 'icons'

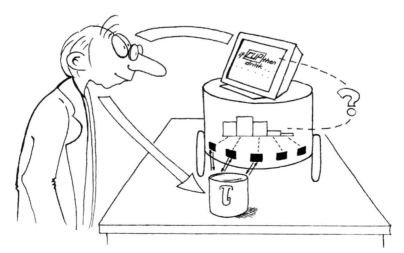

Figure 1. The traditional view of symbol grounding links an *a priori* internal representation (*cup*) to its external referent cup. Reproduced from Figure 3.4, p. 70 of Pfeifer and Scheirer (1999).

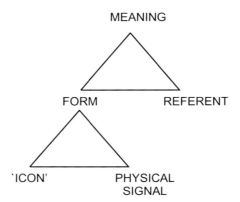

Figure 2. (a) The 'semiotic triangle,' reproduced from Figure 1, p. 433 of Vogt (2002). (b) A more complete picture of symbol grounding in which the form in (a) is grounded by interaction with the physical signal.

in the terminology of Harnad (1990) or 'perceptual symbols' in the terminology of Barsalou (1999). Because these elementary parts result from sensory–motor interaction, we cannot ignore the physics of the world. This leads us to the idea of signal grounding.

Symbol grounding is often discussed in the context of the semiotic triangle as in Figure 2(a), reproduced from Vogt (2002). But as just stated, we believe this picture to be incomplete, since the form is itself symbolic and ungrounded. A more complete view is depicted in Figure 2(b), where interaction with the physical world now grounds the form. In the case of interest here, this interaction is with the speech signal, hence the term 'signal grounding,' which can be seen either as a component part of symbol grounding, or as a specific instance of the SGP, albeit at a lower level than is usually considered. However it is viewed, we believe signal grounding is an indispensable part of symbol grounding.

For example, consider Figure 3. In this particular case of signal grounding, the distal object takes the form of an acoustic speech signal, produced by a vocal tract and perceived through the ear of a listener, linked to an arbitrary and iconic phoneme token (e.g., /æ/ using the notation of the International Phonetic Association, 1999). The form *cat* (or, equivalently, /kæt/) is then composed in a way that is systematic, but nonetheless arbitrary, from these phonemic primitives. Signal grounding then presents numerous challenges when considering the practicalities of forming an equivalence class for the phoneme /æ/. We need to map a wide range of varied signals onto the same phoneme symbol; the system needs to adapt to linguistic change over time; and the grounding of these arbitrary tokens needs to be shared among a population of speakers. These challenges will be taken up in the remainder of the paper.

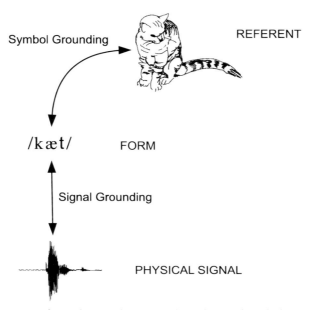

Figure 3. Illustration of signal grounding as a sub-problem of symbol grounding.

To conclude this section, we remark that the ideas of signal and symbol grounding developed here are strongly related to notions of *double articulation*, stemming from the work of de Saussure (1983), which views a linguistic system as a series of differences of sound combined with a series of differences of ideas. At the level of the first articulation, meaningful units (morphemes, words) are combined syntactically to convey ideas. At the level of the second articulation, primitive or elementary sound units (phonemes) are combined to form the meaningful units of the first articulation. The level of the second articulation is vital to human language as a fully productive system, because it is the key (loosely quoting Wilhelm von Humboldt) to achieving infinite generativity from finite machinery. Yet this is the level that is typically ignored by the traditional view of the SGP as characterised in Figure 1.

Basic agent architecture and its operation

The kind of signal grounding just described, and argued to be fundamental to human speech and language as a fully generative system, is a feature of the multi-agent simulation work of Oudeyer. We will take his work as the basis for extensions aimed at producing more realistic sound systems, by defining a *contour space* which acts as an objective function embodying measures of both articulatory

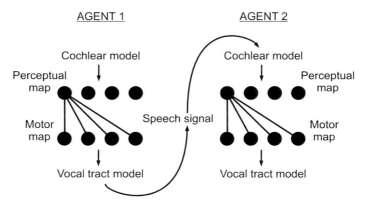

Figure 4. Architecture of the communicating multi-agent system, illustrated here for two agents. Redrawn from Figure 2, p. 439 of Oudeyer (2005c).

effort and phonetic distinctiveness, broadly in line with both H&H theory (Lindblom, 1990) and dispersion-focalisation theory (Schwartz et al., 1997).

Figure 4 shows the basic agent architecture as used by Oudeyer and in this work. Each agent has an artificial ear (cochlear model), an artificial vocal tract, and in Oudeyer's words, an artificial 'brain.' Following Guenter and Gjaja (1996), the 'brain' features two coupled self-organising maps (SOMs, see Kohonen, 1990) — a perceptual map taking input from the auditory system and a motor map driving the articulatory system. Each agent perceives sounds produced by other agents as well as by itself. The appendix sets out details of the cochlear, vocal tract and neural models used by Oudeyer, and in our replications of his work. Note that we have used the "realistic" nonlinear articulatory/acoustic mapping (Oudeyer's Section 6.2) rather than the "abstract" linear mapping (Oudeyer's Section 6.1) throughout.

Our simulations use 10 agents (as compared to the 20 used by Oudeyer). But as he says of the number of agents, "This is a noncritical parameter of the simulations since nothing changes when we tune this parameter, except the speed of convergence of the system" (p. 443). Each 'speaking' agent is 'heard' by just one 'listening' agent (as shown in Figure 4) picked at random. Oudeyer states that "nothing changes" (p. 443) if a speaking agent is heard by more than one listener.

Initially, each agent produces utterances as dictated by its randomly-initialised 'brain' and also perceives the utterances of others. This, over some iterations, causes its SOMs to move from an unstable random configuration to a stable, converged, state of equilibrium. This process of convergence is driven by positive feedback (the basic self-organisation mechanism of the SOM), as each agent becomes increasingly likely to repeat the utterances that it has heard. Eventually, each SOM becomes partitioned into a variable number of basins of attraction as the nodes

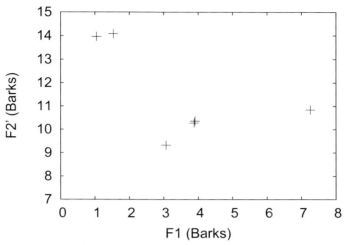

Figure 5. Convergence of Oudeyer's model to a five-vowel system with 10 agents, σ=0.05 and 2,000 iterations. Each cross represents a vector in auditory space; multiple vectors in the same region of space represent an equivalence class, or vowel. For a given equivalence class, individual vectors frequently overlay, giving the appearance of a single cross.

cluster around points of stability — determined by the utterances of the whole population. Any utterance which falls within the range of one of these basins of attraction is perceived by strong activation of the nodes around the centre point, so classifying a wide range of utterances.

The width of each SOM's gaussian function (σ in equation (5) of Appendix 3) determines the size of the basin of attraction and, therefore, in the case of the auditory map, the variety of stimuli perceived as the 'same' utterance. In Oudeyer's simulations, there is no dispersive force and, thus, as σ increases, convergence is to a single point. To quote (Oudeyer, p. 445), "if two neuron clusters… get too close, then the summation of tuning functions in the iterative process of coding/decoding smooths their distribution locally and only one attractor appears." This is not realistic behaviour within a language. However, it is clear that, with the right parameter settings, it is perfectly possible to cause the emergence of a feasible, shared, multi-vowel system. See for instance Figure 5, which depicts a typical result from our replication of Oudeyer's simulation. Here, 500 points initially distributed randomly in F1-F2 space have converged to just five clusters. In fact, in the absence of a dispersive force, the 'clusters' have actually converged (almost) to overlay at the centre of their respective basin of attraction. In the remainder of this paper, we will introduce a dispersive force and study its effect on convergence to linguistically-realistic vowel systems.

Contour spaces

In this section, we introduce basic ideas of H&H theory (Lindblom, 1990) and DFT (Schwartz et al., 1997) into our simulations. According to H&H theory, speakers "tune their performance according to communicative and situation demands… to vary their output along a continuum of *hyper-* and *hypospeech*" (Lindblom, 1990, p. 403). That is, in difficult communication conditions, speakers hyper-articulate in order to be understood, even though this requires additional energy be expended. In less demanding situations, energy can be conserved by hypo-articulation, always provided communication success is maintained. The 'setting' on the hyper-/hypo- continuum is determined by an on-line process in which the speaker continuously infers success of communication by monitoring linguistic and paralinguistic feedback from the listener. We assume that similar forces are at work in the process of vowel formation among a collection of communicating agents; that is, there is not only a drive towards distinctive sound categories (loosely corresponding to 'hyper'), but also an inbuilt desire to minimise energy expended by the agent (loosely corresponding to 'hypo').

Similar ideas are embodied in dispersion-focalisation theory, which encompasses more or less the same principles as H&H theory, but formulated in the auditory (rather than articulatory) domain. This theory seeks to explain the formation of vowel inventories not so much in terms of energy expended by a speaker as via competing forces of "global dispersion based on inter-vowel distances; and local focalization, which is based on intra-vowel spectral salience" (Schwartz et al., 1997, p. 255). The dispersive force thus seeks to maintain distinctiveness between sound categories. The focalisation force in DFT is a little harder to visualise and justify. Is is based on the 'compactness' of formant frequencies, formants being the resonant frequencies of the vocal tract that correspond to "concentration of acoustic energy, reflecting the way that air from the lungs vibrates in the vocal tract, as it changes its shape" (Crystal, 1980, p. 150). These concentrations of energy are reflected in peaks in the frequency spectrum; the one occurring at the lowest frequency is called the first formant, $F1$; that occurring at the next highest frequency is called the second formant, $F2$, and so on.

In the words of Schwartz et al. (1997) (note the minor difference in notation for formant frequencies):

> "a discrimination experiment involving stimuli with various F_2-F_3-F_4 patterns… demonstrated that patterns with the greatest formant convergence (namely with F_3 close to either F_2 or F_4) were more stable in auditory memory… while patterns with less convergence, namely with F_3 at an equal distance from both F_2 and F_4, were more difficult to memorize (Schwartz and Escudier, 1989)." (p. 259)

Schwartz et al. (1997) further note, "the perceptual demonstration that formant convergence in the F_2-F_3-F_4 pattern produced more stable patterns in discrimination experiments, led us to propose that formant convergence could result in an increased 'perceptual value'... because of 'acoustic salience'" (p. 259). Hence, the focalisation force is designed to favour vowels in which the formants are close together in frequency.

Introducing Dispersive Forces

In the long term, we are seeking to minimise the articulatory effort of an utterance, at the same time maximising its perceptual distinctiveness to other agents. At this stage, however, we have no direct way to quantify articulatory effort; hence, we address the problem by using the established ideas of dispersion-focalisation theory (working in the auditory domain as opposed to the articulatory domain), as just discussed. In grounding terms, the drive for perceptual distinctiveness is important in shaping the coupled production-perceptual system. The higher the perceptual distinctiveness, the clearer the meaning of the utterance. When the topological space of our self-organising maps is augmented with dispersion based on inter-vowel differences (in addition to focalisation based on intra-vowel attraction), we refer to it as a *contour space*. By introducing the proposed contour spaces, we hope to achieve a greater robustness to parameter variation and a greater level of realism in the vowel systems that are produced.

We now describe how a repulsive force acting on the perceptual neurons of the agent is introduced. For each node i of the auditory map, at time t, we define an energy functional given by

$$E\left(v_i(t), v_j(t)\right) = \sum_{\substack{j=1 \\ j \neq i}}^{N} \frac{1}{d_{ij}^2} \tag{1}$$

$$\text{where} \quad d_{ij} = \sqrt{\left(F1_i - F1_j\right)^2 + \left(F2'_i - F2'_j\right)^2}$$

In equation (1), j is an index over all N nodes in the auditory map, $v_i = (F1_i, F2'_i)$ and similarly $v_j = (F1_j, F2'_j)$. (Appendix 2 for discussion of $F2'$.) This amounts to a measure of distance between the i and j vowels in the $F1$-$F2'$ auditory-map space.

Updating occurs as follows. At time t, for each neuron i in the auditory space, we generate 8 'test positions' around that neuron. These are spaced on a rectangular grid of side σ centred on i. The update equation is:

$$v_i(t+1) = v_i(t) + \gamma v_{\text{max}} \tag{2}$$

where v_{max} is the $v_k(t)$ vector for which the energy $E(v_i(t),v_k(t))$ is maximised, with k being an index over the 8 neighbours of $v_i(t)$, and γ is a step size or learning rate. Thus, maximisation is performed by gradient ascent. In this way, we are moving the ith vowel in the direction that maximises the acoustic distinctiveness between it and all other vowels in the space.

Attractive Force: Focalisation

The articulatory space is three-dimensional, defined in terms of lip rounding r, tongue position p and tongue height h. As previously discussed, focalisation in our model follows Schwartz et al. (1997) in seeking to favour vowels with compact $F2$-$F3$-$F4$ formant patterns by defining and minimising an energy functional.

The specific energy functional used is similar to that of Schwartz et al. (1997) (see their equations (4) to (7)) modified to fit our simulations using a self-organising map:

$$E(v_l(t) = (r_l, p_l, h_l)) = E_{12} + E_{23} + E_{34} \tag{3}$$

$$\text{where} \qquad E_{12} = -\left(\frac{1}{(F2_l - F1_l)^2}\right)$$

$$E_{23} = -\left(\frac{1}{(F3_l - F2_l)^2}\right)$$

$$E_{34} = -\left(\frac{1}{(F4_l - F3_l)^2}\right)$$

In (3), each neuron l has its associated (r_l, p_l, h_l) values, which allow computation of formant values via the vocal tract model (Appendix 1). At time t, each such neuron has its vector $v_l(t)$ updated according to:

$$v_l(t+1) = v_l(t) + \gamma v_{min} \tag{4}$$

where v_{min} is the $v_m(t)$ vector for which $E(v_m(t))$ is minimised, m is an index over the 26 neighbours of $v_l(t)$ (on a grid of size σ in 3-D space), and γ is a step size or learning rate. Hence, we are minimising by gradient descent.

Note that although this mechanism of attraction is firmly based in perception, we are in fact minimising in (r,p,h) space. Hence, we view this as, effectively, a mechanism for reducing (if not actually minimising) articulatory effort in line with H&H theory.

Results of simulations

In this section, we first show some typical illustrative results obtained using Oudeyer's model to act as a benchmark before presenting typical results from the new model based on DFT. Thereafter, more thorough results (averaged over 500 runs) are given comparing the sensitivity of the two models to variation in the gaussian width parameter, σ. The two models are also compared with respect to the emergence of realistic vowel systems (i.e., their similarity to those observed in human languages). In all simulations, the nodes of the self-organising maps are initially randomised, that is, placed at uniformly-distributed positions in the appropriate space.

In these simulations, the optimisation step size, γ of equations (2) and (4), is set equal to the gaussian width, σ of equation (5) in Appendix 3, enabling all three forces (i.e., dispersion, focalisation, self-organisation) to maintain their intended, relative level of influence. The gaussian width in the auditory space was scaled up to take account of the different range of the two maps ($[0,1]^3$ for the motor map and [0..8 Bark, 0..15 Bark] for the auditory map). All SOMs have 500 nodes, and simulations are stopped after 2,000 iterations of two-agent interaction. This stopping criterion was decided after examining how auditory dispersion (measured from the energy functional of eqn. (1)) varied during a few trials of the simulation. Figure 6 depicts a typical example. Although dispersion does not reduce monotonically, convergence is achieved well before 2,000 iterations.

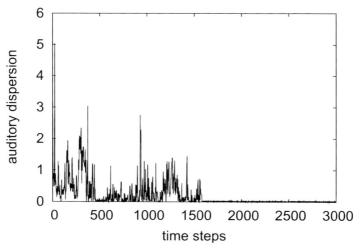

Figure 6. Typical plot of auditory dispersion versus number of iterations, showing convergence well before 2,000 steps.

Reproduction of Oudeyer's Results

We have already shown an example of how the initial model can converge to a reasonable five-vowel system with $\sigma = 0.05$ (Figure 5 earlier). We have also detailed how, as σ increases, there is a strong tendency to converge to a single point. Fig-

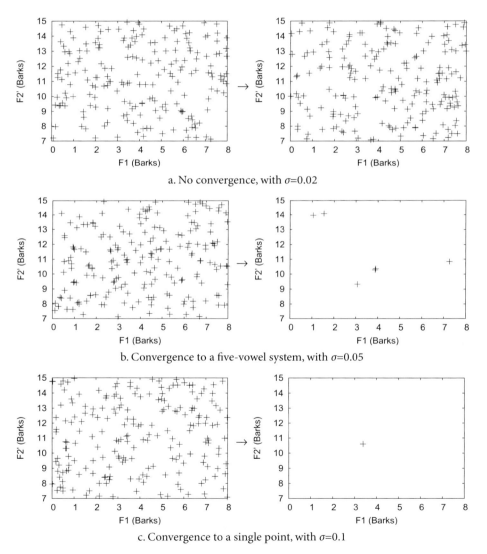

Figure 7. Composite of typical results from our replication of Oudeyer's simulation as σ varies.

ure 7 shows a composite of typical results as σ varies. It is seen that realistic vowel systems emerge only for a restricted range of σ values.

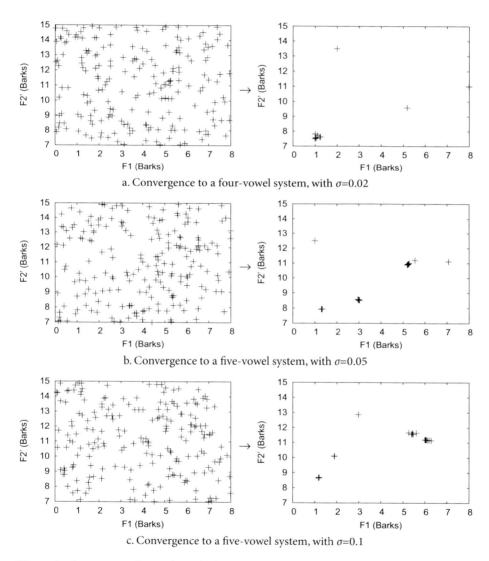

Figure 8. Composite of typical results from simulations of the new model with contour spaces with the same σ values as in Figure 7. Realistic vowel systems emerge over a much wider range of σ values.

Effect of the Contour Space

Figure 8 shows a composite of typical results from simulations of the new model with contour spaces with the same σ values as in Figure 7. As can be clearly seen, realistic vowel systems emerge over a much wider range of σ values. There is also, we think, less tendency for the converged points to overlay exactly than in the original work (i.e., there is more of a 'cluster').

Further comparison of the two systems

To test further the assertion that the new system featuring dispersive forces (i.e., contour spaces) will possess a greater robustness to parameter variation than Oudeyer's original, 500 repeated runs were made for different values of the gaussian width σ. The number of vowels present after convergence was then recorded for both systems. If convergence did not occur, results were discarded. Figure 9 shows the results averaged over the 500 runs; the error bars depict the standard deviation.

For the new system, a high level of variation in the number of vowels observed at convergence is seen across the whole range of σ values. We take this to be a positive feature of the new system, since human languages display a wide variety of vowel inventories (Maddieson, 1984; Ladefoged and Maddieson, 1996). By contrast, the Oudeyer system (as replicated by us) shows unrealistic convergence to a single 'vowel' with zero variability for $\sigma > 0.07$ and a total lack of convergence (to a

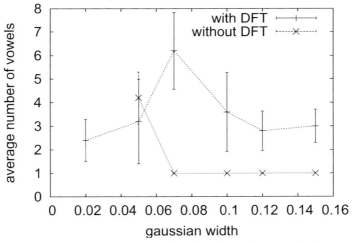

Figure 9. Comparison of our replication of Oudeyer's simulation with the new model based on DFT, illustrating the robustness to parameter variation resulting from inclusion of a dispersive force. Error bars are standard deviations over 500 runs.

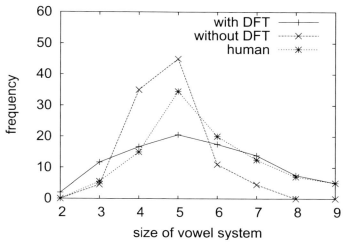

Figure 10. Comparison of vowel systems observed in human languages and those produced by computer simulation with and without DFT (i.e., with and without dispersive
forces).

sensibly small number of clusters) for $\sigma < 0.05$. Realistic convergence is maintained
for the new system up to parameter values of 0.15. No simulations were performed
for $\sigma > 0.15$.

Following Oudeyer (2005c, Figure 10, p. 446), we have also compared the two
systems with data for human languages, taking vowel frequencies from Ladefoged
and Maddieson (1996). For the new computer model, σ was set to 0.05 and 500
simulations were run. Comparative data for Oudeyer's system for the same value
of σ and number of iterations were taken from his original paper, rather than the
simulations being replicated here. Figure 10 shows the comparison, which reveals
that the system with contour spaces has a slight preference for simpler vowel systems but is able to capture the emergence of the more complex systems, which is
a problem for Oudeyer. Quantitatively, the mean square error (MSE) between the
curve for Oudeyer's data (labelled "without DFT") and the human data is 91.28,
whereas the corresponding MSE for our simulations (labelled "with DFT") is 29.94.
All three systems share a peak of five vowels. We emphasise that this comparison
is made under conditions (namely, σ set at 0.05) which are maximally favourable
to Oudeyer's model. This is necessary because of the sensitivity of his model to the
setting of σ.

Discussion and Conclusions

The tension introduced by the addition of a dispersive force has clearly had a beneficial effect. This extension achieves an increased level of robustness to parameter variation and captures the emergence of some of the more complex vowel systems observed in human languages, in a way which Oudeyer was unable to do. Despite a slight preference for the simpler vowel systems, the distribution is more representative of that seen in real languages, as confirmed by the much lower mean square error (see previous section).

How have these beneficial effects come about? Boë, Schwartz and Vallée (1994) have already shown, although not in a multi-agent setting, how DFT can produce a range of vowel systems. (Rather, starting with a full set of vowel 'prototypes,' they show how DFT can be used to select realistic subsets typical of different languages.) In the present setting, the three forces of dispersion, focalisation and self-organisation act to produce convergence to attractors in the contour space. These attractors correspond to a physical grounding of the speech signals produced by the agents, as in Figure 2(b). The gradual, progressive nature of the convergence, over many interactions, ensures the final set of signal-grounded forms is shared among the population. So the physics governing a population not only potentially accounts for a wide variety of human vowel systems but also allows for this set to become established within a population.

In our work, grounding of the external world is via these attractors in contour space. So, rather than connecting an arbitrary *a priori* abstraction (as when *cat* in the environment is miraculously labelled 'cat' in one bound), we are connecting a more complete representation of the distal object, built on the physics of the situation. Through the formation of attractors, we have both a clear shared abstraction, its centre point, and a basin of attraction capturing the ambiguity and differences present in the real world. We feel that this view can answer some of the current criticisms of the symbol grounding paradigm (e.g., Lakoff, 1993), because the attractors capture the ambiguities and 'shades of grey' that challenge more traditional views of grounding (Davidsson, 1993). This has similarities to previous work which has sought to explain grounding using connectionist models (e.g., Harnad, 1993; Damper and Harnad, 2000; Cangelosi, Greco and Harnad, 2002). These have been successful in displaying various aspects of human cognition. But, by considering grounding at the (sub-form) level of physical signals (Figures 2(b) and 3), we have developed a new framework in which this interplay between symbol grounding and connectionist systems can be further explored.

Several possibilities for future work are under consideration. At present, agents do not exactly 'hear' sounds; rather, they have direct access to formant values. From

*F*1, *F*2, *F*3 and *F*4 values specifying a vocalisation, they perceive *F*1 directly and compute a perceived *F*2′. This is a very high level of abstraction, implicitly making many assumptions (e.g., about the role of formants in speech perception, and how the auditory system can extract them from the speech signal). First and foremost, therefore, we wish to move to using actual sounds as the medium of interchange between agents. This move will make it necessary to use more physically realistic vocal tract and cochlear models. It is then a matter of some importance and interest to investigate how much increased realism/complexity impacts on the emergence of sound systems. We know from Oudeyer and the present work that very simple, highly abstract models are adequate for the production of shared (static) vowel systems, but under rather strong assumptions. Furthermore, speech sounds do not consist entirely of vowels, but of dynamic consonant-vowel patterns forming syllables. Unfortunately, although there is general agreement among phoneticians and speech scientists that vowels can be reasonably well specified by formant values, there is no corresponding understanding of how consonant sounds can be similarly specified and distinguished.

Although Oudeyer (2005b) has extended his "abstract" linear model in the direction of "the formation of… and patterns of sound combination" (p. 328), this is done without any acoustic, perceptual space, but with agents given direct access to the relevant parameters in what we believe to be an unsatisfactory ('mind-reading') manner. By moving to simulations in which actual, physical speech sounds are exchanged between agents, we can hope to explore the emergence of speech as a dynamic phenomenon in a more realistic and satisfactory way.

References

Barsalou, L. W. (1999). Perceptual symbol systems. *Behavioral and Brain Sciences, 22*(4), 577–609.

Boë, L.-J., Schwartz, J.-L., and Vallée, N. (1994). The prediction of vowel systems: Perceptual contrast and stability. In E. Keller (Ed.), *Fundamentals of speech synthesis and speech recognition* (pp. 185–213). Chichester, UK: John Wiley.

Brooks, R. A. (1990). Elephants don't play chess. *Robotics and Autonomous Systems, 6*(1), 3–15.

Brooks, R. A. (1991). Intelligence without representation. *Artificial Intelligence, 47*(1–3), 139–159.

Brooks, R. A. (1999). *Cambrian intelligence*. Cambridge, MA: Bradford Books/MIT Press.

Cangelosi, A., Greco, A., and Harnad, S. (2002). Symbol grounding and the symbolic theft hypothesis. In A. Cangelosi and D. Parisi (Eds.), *Simulating the evolution of language* (pp. 191–210). London, UK: Springer-Verlag.

Carlson, R., Granström, B., and Fant, G. (1970). Some studies concerning perception of isolated vowels. *STL-QPSR, 2–3*, 19–35.

Chistovich, L. A., and Lublinskaya, V. V. (1979). The 'centre of gravity' effect in vowel spectra and critical distance between the formants: Psychoacoustic study of the perception of vowel-like stimuli. *Hearing Research, 1*(3), 185–195.

Crystal, D. (1980). *A first dictionary of linguistics and phonetics*. London: André Deutsch.

Damper, R. I. (2000). Emergence and levels of abstraction. *International Journal of Systems Science, 31*(7), 811–818.

Damper, R. I., and Harnad, S. R. (2000). Neural network models of categorical perception. *Perception and Psychophysics, 62*(4), 843–867.

Davidsson, P. (1993). Toward a general solution to the symbol grounding problem: Combining machine learning and computer vision. In *Fall symposium series, machine learning in computer vision: What, why and how?* (pp. 157–161). Raleigh, NC.

de Boer, B. (2000). Self-organization in vowel systems. *Journal of Phonetics, 28*(4), 441–465.

de Boer, B. (2001). *The origins of vowel systems*. Oxford, UK: Oxford University Press.

de Boer, B. (2005). Evolution of speech and its acquistion. *Adaptive Behavior, 13*(4), 281–292.

de Saussure, F. (1983). *Course in general linguistics*. London, UK: Duckworth. (Translation of 1916 edition by R. Harris)

Dietrich, E. (1990). Computationalism. *Social Epistemology, 4*(2), 135–154.

Fodor, J. (1975). *The language of thought*. New York, NY: Crowell.

Guenter, F. H., and Gjaja, M. N. (1996). The perceptual magnet effect as an emergent property of neural map formation. *Journal of the Acoustical Society of America, 100*(2), 1111–1121.

Harnad, S. (1990). The symbol grounding problem. *Physica D, 42*, 335–346.

Harnad, S. (1993). Grounding symbols in the analog world with neural nets. *Think, 2*(1), 12–78.

Haugeland, J. (1985). *Artificial intelligence: The very idea*. Cambridge, MA: Bradford Books/MIT Press.

International Phonetic Association. (1999). *Handbook of the international phonetic association: A guide to the use of the international phonetic alphabet*. Cambridge, UK: Cambridge University Press.

Kirby, S. (2001). Spontaneous evolution of linguistic structure: An iterated learning model of the emergence of regularity and irregularity. *IEEE Transactions on Evolutionary Computation, 5*(2), 102–110.

Kirby, S., and Hurford, J. (2002). The emergence of linguistic structure: An overview of the iterated learning model. In A. Cangelosi and D. Parisi (Eds.), *Simulating the evolution of language* (pp. 121–148). London, UK: Springer-Verlag.

Kohonen, T. (1990). The self-organising map. *Proceedings of the IEEE, 78*(9), 1464–1480.

Ladefoged, P., and Maddieson, I. (1996). *The sounds of the world's languages*. Oxford, UK: Blackwell Scientific Publishers.

Lakoff, G. (1993). Grounded concepts without symbols. In *Proceedings of the fifteenth annual meeting of the cognitive society* (pp. 161–164). Boulder, CO.

Liljencrantz, J., and Lindblom, B. (1972). Numerical simulations of vowel quality systems: The role of perceptual contrast. *Language, 48*, 839–862.

Lindblom, B. (1986). Phonetic universals in vowel systems. In J. J. Ohala and J. J. Jaeger (Eds.), *Experimental phonology* (pp. 14–44). Orlando, FL: Academic Press.

Lindblom, B. (1990). Explaining phonetic variation: A sketch of H&H theory. In W. J. Hardcastle and A. Marchal (Eds.), *Speech production and speech modelling* (pp. 403–439). Dordrecht, The Netherlands: Kluwer Academic Publishers.

Lindblom, B. (2000). Developmental origins of adult phonology: The interplay between phonetic emergents and the evolutionary adaptation of sound patterns. *Phonetica, 57*(2–4), 297–314.

Lindblom, B., MacNeilage, P., and Studdert-Kennedy, M. (1984). Self-organizing processes and the explanation of phonological universals. In B. Butterworth, B. Comrie, and Ö. Dahl (Eds.), *Explanations for language universals* (pp. 181–203). New York, NY: Mouton.

Maddieson, I. (1984). *Patterns of sounds.* Cambridge, UK: Cambridge University Press.

Mays, W. (1951). The hypothesis of cybernetics. *British Journal for the Philosophy of Science, 2*(7), 249–250.

Minsky, M. (1974). *A framework for representing knowledge* (Tech. Rep. Nos. AIM–306). Cambridge, MA: Artificial Intelligence Laboratory, Massachusetts Institute of Technology.

Minsky, M. (1990). Analogical vs. logical or symbolic vs. connectionist or neat vs. scruffy. In P. H. Winston (Ed.), *Artificial intelligence at mit: Epanding frontiers* (Vol. 1, pp. 219–243). Cambridge, MA: MIT Press.

Newell, A. (1973). Artificial intelligence and the concept of mind. In R. C. Shank and K. M. Colby (Eds.), *Computer models of thought and language* (pp. 1–60). San Francisco, CA: Freeman.

Newell, A. (1980). Physical symbol systems. *Cognitive Science, 4*(2), 135–183.

Newell, A. (1990). *Unified theories of cognition.* Cambridge, MA: Harvard University Press.

Newell, A., and Simon, H. (1976). Computer science as empirical inquiry: Symbols and search. *Communications of the ACM, 19*(3), 113–126.

Oudeyer, P.-Y. (2005a). How phonological structures can be culturally selected for learnability. *Adaptive Behavior, 13*(4), 269–280.

Oudeyer, P.-Y. (2005b). The self-organization of combinatoriality and phonotactics in vocalization systems. *Connection Science, 17*(3–4), 325–341.

Oudeyer, P.-Y. (2005c). The self-organization of speech sounds. *Journal of Theoretical Biology, 233*(3), 435–449.

Pfeifer, R., and Scheirer, C. (1999). *Understanding intelligence.* Cambridge, MA: MIT Press.

Pylyshyn, Z. W. (1984). *Computation and cognition: Toward a foundation for cognitive science.* Cambridge, MA: Bradford Books/MIT Press.

Schwartz, J.-L., Boë, L.-J., Vallée, N., and Abry, C. (1997). The dispersion-focalization theory of vowel systems. *Journal of Phonetics, 25*(3), 255–286.

Schwartz, J.-L., and Escudier, P. (1989). A strong evidence for the existence of a large scale integrated spectral representation in vowel perception. *Speech Communication, 8*(3), 235–259.

Steels, L. (1997). The synthetic modeling of language origins. *Evolution of Communication, 1*(1), 1–35.

Steels, L. (1998). The origins of syntax in visually grounded robotic agents. *Artificial Intelligence, 103*(1–2), 133–156.

Steels, L. (1999). *The talking heads experiment. volume 1: Words and meanings.* Antwerpen, Belgium: Laboratorium.

Steels, L. (2003). Evolving grounded communication for robots. *Trends in Cognitive Science, 7*(7), 308–312.

Sun, R. (2000). Symbol grounding: A new look at an old idea. *Philosophical Psychology, 13*(2), 149–172.

Traunmüller, H. (1990). Analytical expressions for the tonotopic sensory scale. *Journal of the Acoustical Society of America, 88*(1), 97–100.

Vogt, P. (2002). The physical symbol grounding problem. *Cognitive Systems Research, 3*(3), 429–457.

Appendix: Oudeyer's Agent Model

In Oudeyer's work, each agent has an artificial vocal tract, an artificial ear (cochlear model), and an artificial 'brain', or neural model. These will now be detailed in turn.

1. Vocal Tract Model

Following de Boer (2001), Oudeyer uses a vocal tract simulation controlled by three parameters, namely lip rounding r, tongue height h and tongue position p. Each parameter is constrained to reflect the anatomical range of the corresponding articulator movement. We can derive formant values as follows:

$$
\begin{aligned}
F1 &= ((-392+392r)h^2 + (596-668r)h + (-146+166r))p^2 + ((348-348r)h^2 \\
&\quad + (-494+606r)h + (141-175r))p + ((340-72r)h^2 + (-796+108r)h \\
&\quad + (708-38r)) \\
F2 &= ((-1200+1208r)h^2 + (1320-1328r)h + (118-158r))p^2 \\
&\quad + ((1864-1488r)h^2 + (-2644+1510r)h + (-561+221r))p \\
&\quad + ((-670+490r)h^2 + (1355-697r)h + (1517-117r)) \\
F3 &= ((604-604r)h^2 + (1038-1178r)h + (246+566r))p^2 + ((-1150+1262r)h^2 \\
&\quad + (-1443+1313r)h + (-317-483r))p + ((1130-836r)h^2 \\
&\quad + (-315+44r)h + (2427-127r)) \\
F4 &= ((-1120+16r)h^2 + (1696-180r)h + (500+522r))p^2 + ((-140+240r)h^2 \\
&\quad + (-578+214r)h + (-692-419r))p + ((1480-602r)h^2 \\
&\quad + (-1220+289r)h + (3678-178r))
\end{aligned}
$$

Although it would be possible to produce sounds (i.e., synthetic vowels) exhibiting these formant values, which were then 'heard' by the 'speaker' and other agents, this is not done in Oudeyer's simulations or in ours. Rather, a short-cut is taken in which auditory parameters are calculated from the formant values.

2. Cochlear Model

A cochlear (ear) model, designed by Boë, Schwartz and Vallée (1994), is employed to process the formant values, placing the result in a 2-D auditory space. The model perceives the first formant directly and derives an 'effective' second formant, $F2'$ (Carlson, Granström and Fant, 1970), as follows:

$$
F2' = \begin{cases}
F2 & \text{if } F3-F2>c \\
\frac{(2-w_1)F2+w_1F3}{2} & \text{if } F3-F2\leq c \text{ and } F4-F2\geq c \\
\frac{w_2F2+(2-w_2)F3}{2}-1 & \text{if } F4-F2\leq c \text{ and } F3-F2\leq F4-F3 \\
\frac{(2+w_2)F3-w_2F4}{2}-1 & \text{if } F4-F2\leq c \text{ and } F3-F2\geq F4-F3).
\end{cases}
$$

where c is as a constant of value 3.5 Bark (Chistovich and Lublinskaya, 1979), and w_1 and w_2 are defined as:

$$w_1 = \frac{c - (F3 - F2)}{c}$$

$$w_2 = \frac{(F4 - F3) - (F3 - F2)}{F4 - F2}$$

The above equations assume frequency is represented on the Bark scale. Conversion to this scale from hertz frequency is done using the following conversion formula (Traunmüller, 1990):

$$f_{Bark} = \frac{26.81}{1 + 1960/f_{Hz}} - 0.53$$

3. Neural Model

The neural model is based on two self-organising maps (Kohonen, 1990). The self-organising map (SOM) defining the articulatory space captures the configurations of the vocal tract in terms of parameters r, h and p. The auditory space codes for the range of acoustic cues in terms of the first formant $F1$ and second 'effective' formant $F2'$. Each agent's neural model is then established by forming weighted connections between the nodes of the auditory and articulatory spaces.

When activated, the jth node in the articulatory space produces a vector $v_j = (r_j, h_j, p_j)$ forming a point in $[0,1]^3$ space coding articulatory configuration. A sequence of these vectors, $v_1, v_2, ..., v_n$ where n is a random number between 2 and 4, is then fed to the vocal tract model. This produces an articulatory trajectory ('utterance') of from 2 to 4 configurations. All remaining neurons are then modified according to:

$$v_k(t+1) = v_k(t) + G_k(v_j)(v_j - v_k(t)) \quad \begin{cases} k = 1..N, k \neq j, \\ \text{where } N \text{ is the number of neurons in each map} \end{cases}$$

Each articulatory neuron is updated by a gaussian activation function:

$$G_k(v_j) = \exp\left(\frac{d_{j,k}^2}{2\sigma^2}\right) \tag{5}$$

$$\text{where } d_{j,k}^2 = |v_j - v_k|^2$$

This update mechanism causes the nodes to converge on points in the articulatory space. The location of these points of convergence is determined by the agent's choice of articulation and the utterances that it is exposed to. The articulatory space can then be modified by the auditory space through the weighted connections between the two. The connections between the perceptual neuron i and the articulatory neuron j are characterised by the weight $w_{i,j}$ (initially random).

The auditory space is able to achieve a similar convergence, since on perceiving an utterance a vector containing acoustic cues s (derived from the 'speech signal') is placed in the perceptual space and the neurons updated by:

$$v_i(t+1) = v_i(t) + G_i(s)(s - v_i(t))$$

The articulatory space is then further updated through the weighted connections by characterising $d_{j,k}^2$ as:

$$d_{j,k}^2 = \sum_{i}^{N} w_{i,j} G_i(s)$$

Taking the function dependence of $G(\ )$ on s as implicit, for simplicity, the weights are updated by a Hebbian learning rule:

$$\Delta w_{i,j} = \alpha (G_i - \langle G_i \rangle)(G_j - \langle G_j \rangle)$$

where α is set to some small random number and $\langle G_j \rangle$ represents the average gaussian activation over the previous time steps.

Social symbol grounding and language evolution

Paul Vogt[1] and Federico Divina[1,2]
[1]ILK / Communication and Information Science, Tilburg University,
The Netherlands / [2]School of Engineering, Pablo de Olavide University,
Seville, Spain

This paper illustrates how external (or *social*) symbol grounding can be studied in simulations with large populations. We discuss how we can simulate language evolution in a relatively complex environment which has been developed in the context of the New Ties project. This project has the objective of evolving a cultural society and, in doing so, the agents have to evolve a communication system that is grounded in their interactions with their virtual environment and with other individuals. A preliminary experiment is presented in which we investigate the effect of a number of learning mechanisms. The results show that the social symbol grounding problem is a particularly hard one; however, we provide an ideal platform to study this problem.

Keywords: agent based modelling, language evolution, referential indeterminacy, joint attention, principle of contrast, cross-situational learning

Introduction

Human language is thought to have evolved from an interaction among three adaptive systems: biological evolution, individual learning and cultural evolution (Kirby & Hurford, 2002). The New Ties project[1] aims to merge these systems in a large scale simulation to evolve a cultural society of simulated agents that are situated in a complex environment and that need to acquire behaviours to remain viable over extended periods of time. One important aspect of this simulation is to evolve language that allows social learning, while being grounded in a virtual world.

The symbol grounding problem (Harnad, 1990) has been studied in relation to both language acquisition and language evolution using various robotic models (e.g., Roy, 2005; Steels, Kaplan, McIntyre, & Van Looveren, 2002; Vogt, 2002) and related simulations (e.g., Steels & Belpaeme, 2005; Cangelosi, 2001; A. D. M. Smith,

2005; Vogt, 2005). For overviews, see, for example, Cangelosi and Parisi (2002) or Vogt (2006). Most of these studies have focused on the ability of (simulated) robots to construct a shared symbolic communication system that has no 'survival' function to the society (but see, e.g., Cangelosi, 2001, for an exception). Such a survival function, however, is a crucial aspect of symbol grounding (Ziemke & Sharkey, 2001). The New Ties project will focus on how a language can evolve in a way that is relevant to the society's survival. To this end we need to deal with what Cangelosi (2006) has called *social symbol grounding*, that is, symbol grounding in (potentially large) populations.

To arrive at a shared set of symbolic conventions, the agents have to learn language from each other. In doing that, they face a problem that is closely related to the *referential indeterminacy* problem illustrated by Quine (1960). Quine showed that when learning a new word, the word can have — logically speaking — an infinite number of meanings. He used the example of an anthropologist who is studying a native speaker of a — to him — unknown language. When a rabbit suddenly scurries by, the native exclaims "gavagai!" and the anthropologist notes that gavagai means rabbit. Although this may be a valid inference, gavagai could also have meant undetached rabbit parts, dinner, running animal or even it's going to rain. To reduce the number of possible meanings, the anthropologist has to acquire more information regarding the meaning of gavagai. People — especially children — are extremely good at this, but for robots this has proven to be a very hard problem (Vogt, 2006).

Inspired by the literature on children's language acquisition, several learning mechanisms have been studied using computational models (see, e.g., A. D. M. Smith, 2005; Vogt & Coumans, 2003). Based on such studies, we present a new hybrid model that combines these learning mechanisms, which involve joint attention, feedback, cross-situational learning and the principle of contrast, in one model. We investigate the effect of these learning mechanisms on the ability to evolve a shared language in a large population. The next section provides more background on the symbol grounding problem. After that we present an overview of the New Ties project, followed by a more detailed description of the hybrid model that allows the population to evolve language. This description is followed by the presentation of some experiments investigating the learning mechanisms. The experiments are then discussed in relation to social symbol grounding before the paper concludes.

Symbol grounding

Physical symbol grounding

When agents communicate about things that are relevant in the world, they have to solve the symbol grounding problem (Harnad, 1990). Vogt (2002) has argued that, to achieve this, agents need to construct a semiotic relation between a *referent* (being something concrete or abstract), a *meaning* (being a representation inside an agent's brain that has some function to the agent) and a *form* (being the signal conveyed). This triadic relation (see Figure 1) is what Peirce (1931–1958) has called a symbol, provided the relation between form and meaning is either arbitrary or conventionalised.[2] The hardest part of solving this *physical symbol grounding problem* (i.e., creating the semiotic triangle, Vogt, 2002) is the construction of the relation between referent and meaning, because this relation is often dynamic and complex. As the physical symbol grounding problem may relate only to individual agents, the form could — in principle — be any arbitrary signal or label associated with this relation (Vogt, 2006). However, in language, the forms have to be conventionalised through cultural interactions and communicating forms have to be functional (e.g., it has to invoke some response from the recipient). Hence the population has to deal with *external symbol grounding* (Cowley, 2006), which we interpret as *social symbol grounding* (Cangelosi, 2006), i.e., symbol grounding in populations.

Social symbol grounding

Various studies have shown how a shared system of symbols can evolve from scratch through (local) cultural interactions between agents and (individual) learning mechanisms (Cangelosi, 2001; Steels & Belpaeme, 2005; Vogt, 2002). In this approach, which assumes that language is a *complex adaptive dynamical*

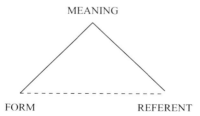

MEANING

FORM   REFERENT

Figure 1. The semiotic triangle indicates the triadic relation among referent, meaning and form. Note that the relation between referent and form is indirect (hence the dotted line). When the relation between meaning and form is either arbitrary or conventionalised, the triangle represents a symbol. (Figure adapted from Ogden & Richards, 1923.)

system (Steels, 1997), a population of agents interact through a long series of *language games*. During these language games, agents can adapt their language, such that a shared structure (the external language) evolves through self-organisation. We believe that crucial aspects in the success of social symbol grounding are cognitive learning mechanisms, non-verbal interactions, physical properties of the environment and population dynamics.

Quine's referential indeterminacy problem can make the social symbol grounding problem more complicated than the physical symbol grounding problem. Many learning mechanisms in developmental linguistics have been proposed to deal with this problem (see, e.g. Bloom, 2000, for an overview). For instance, Tomasello (1999) has proposed that *joint attention* is a crucial mechanism by which two interlocutors focus their shared attention on a third object, allowing a child to associate utterances to the same situation the adult is attending to. This way, referential indeterminacy is reduced substantially, though the gavagai example shows this is not sufficient. The anthropologist can infer that gavagai relates to the rabbit, but is it the whole rabbit, its movement, its function, or something else? Additional mechanisms therefore have to be part of the cognitive learning mechanism.

Researchers have proposed a number of additional mechanisms that might further reduce referential indeterminacy, such as, e.g., the *principle of contrast* (Clark, 1993). In addition there is ample, though controversial, evidence that children receive feedback from their caregivers regarding their language use — especially regarding word-meaning mappings (Chouinard & Clark, 2003). Finally, evidence suggests that children may learn some words more straightforwardly by taking the intersection of their possible meanings across situations (Akhtar & Montague, 1999). This process, known as *cross-situational learning*, seems to take place from very early in the development of infants (Houston-Price et al., 2005).

Previous computational studies have investigated some of these mechanisms, but in isolation. Joint attention is most often modelled through *explicit meaning transfer*, where the hearer gets access to the exact intended meaning (e.g., Oliphant & Batali, 1997). More realistically, a number of robotic studies have used pointing as an unreliable joint attention mechanism, so hearers could not exactly determine the intended meaning, but could only estimate the intended referent (Vogt, 2000). In many studies corrective feedback on the referent or meaning has been the prime ingredient of the so-called *guessing games*, which allows agents to acquire the right association and to disambiguate competing word-meaning mappings through lateral inhibition (Steels & Belpaeme, 2005; Steels et al., 2002; Vogt, 2002). Finally, cross-situational learning, which is similar to the guessing game but without feedback, has been investigated extensively in computer models

(Siskind, 1996; A. D. M. Smith, 2005; Vogt, 2000) and mathematical models (K. Smith et al., 2006).

In a study that has compared joint attention, feedback (through explicit meaning transfer) and cross-situational learning, Vogt and Coumans (2003) have found that cross-situational learning is hard to scale up for larger populations. This is because in the early stages of evolution different agents invent different words to convey the same meaning, which then have to be disambiguated during further development in order for effective communication to take place. If there is joint attention or feedback, disambiguation can be performed quite efficiently. However, cross-situational learning is based on the assumption that a word and its meaning are consistently co-occurring in different contexts. If there are many different words for a meaning, more ambiguities can enter the language and this condition may no longer hold. It has been shown, however, that cross-situational learning improves if there are additional biases such as mutual exclusivity (A. D. M. Smith, 2005) or some other synonymy damping mechanism (De Beule et al., 2006).

In the hybrid model that we introduce later, we combine the following mechanisms:

Joint attention is modelled by a pointing mechanism which allows a hearer to identify the target object reliably. This mechanism does not resolve uncertainty about the meaning of an utterance, because this relates to a feature of the object, such as colour or shape.

The principle of contrast allows agents to acquire the meaning of words such that they tend to favour meanings that have not yet been associated with other words.

Feedback is used as a non-verbal signal to indicate whether the hearer 'thinks' it has understood the speaker. Thus, the feedback may be prone to errors. Although negative feedback does not necessarily lead to correction, it increases the chance that the speaker repeats itself while using joint attention.

Cross-situational learning allows the refined learning of correct word-meaning mappings, regardless of whether joint attention is present.

In the simulations reported in this paper, we investigate the effect of each of these mechanisms on the ability to develop a shared lexicon.

New Ties

The objective of this project is to set up a simulation in which a large population of agents (i.e., more than 1,000) can evolve a cultural society using evolutionary, individual and social learning. Sub-objectives include investigating the interaction among these three adaptive systems and evolving a communication system that facilitates social learning. It is the latter aspect which is relevant to social symbol grounding and to this paper. Below is a brief description of the project; for more details consult Gilbert et al. (2006).[3]

The New Ties world — inspired by Epstein and Axtell's (1996) sugar-scape world — is a virtual world with places of varying roughness that contain objects such as tokens, edible plants and agents. Agents are provided with sensors and actuators that allow them to see and act. The sensors are configured such that an agent can see a number of perceptual features (e.g., colour, shape, direction, distance) of the objects in their visual field. The actuators allow the agents to, among others, move forward, turn left or right, eat, mate and talk. Each action costs energy, the amount of which depends, for instance, on the weight carried by the agents. When an agent's energy falls to zero, it dies, but it can also die of old age. Eating plants increases the agent's energy level, which depends on the 'ripeness' of the plant.

Agents develop their own control system using evolutionary, individual and social learning. This control system is a *decision Q-tree* (DQT), which is a stochastic decision tree that may change using reinforcement learning. The details of this DQT are beyond the scope of this paper, and the interested reader is referred to Gilbert et al. (2006). Suffice it to say that the DQT takes categories of perceived objects and interpreted messages as input and outputs an action based on some decision process. The structure of the DQT can change based on cross-over and mutation during reproduction, reinforcement learning and social learning. As we will discuss, social learning allows agents to develop shared behavioural skills using socially grounded symbols.

The genome carries, apart from the initial structure of the controller, a number of biases influencing the behaviours of agents regarding aspects such as the tendency to be social. The social bias is particularly important for language evolution, as it regulates, for instance, the frequency with which agents communicate or assist each other with learning language. Interaction is achieved by the predefined production and interpretation mechanisms, as explained in the next section.

Language evolution in New Ties

Figure 2 shows the architecture of the agents. The architecture consists of four modules, which are processed in sequential order from top to bottom. In addition, each agent has a short term memory (STM) and a long term memory (LTM). The

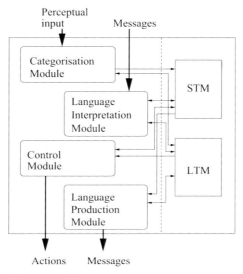

Figure 2. The basic architecture of the agents.

input to an agent includes perceptual input regarding all objects an agent can see in its visual field and all messages sent within its audible range. There is no noise in perception, so it is assumed to be perfect. (Note that agents do not exactly share their visual or audible fields as they cannot be at the same location simultaneously.)

The perceptual input is first sent to the categorisation module, where each feature of each object is categorised with its nearest category. Categories are represented as predefined prototypes stored in the LTM in one-dimensional *conceptual spaces* (Gärdenfors, 2000). Each conceptual space relates to some quality dimension, such as colour, shape, direction, etc. It is possible to specify which categories are predefined and allow other categories to be acquired during development by playing discrimination games similar to the ones described in (Vogt, 2005). In the simulations reported here, the prototypes have a one-to-one relation among all possible perceptual features of all objects in the visual field, and the discrimination game has been switched off.

Since objects are perceived with different features (colour, shape, etc.), categorising an object results in a category set stored in the STM for further processing by other modules. The categories of all objects in the visual field constitute the *context (Cxt)*. The context and interpreted messages are used by the control module to decide on an action to take. These actions can fail if they are in conflict with the 'physical' laws of the environment (e.g., two agents cannot be at the same location simultaneously).

When communicating, the agents construct physically grounded symbols (i.e., the semiotic triangle). With respect to the current setup of the model, the referent is a single perceptual feature of an object (e.g., a colour), the meaning is represented by its category and the form is a single word. For the moment we treat the meaning as a representation that has no real function regarding the agents' life task, though interpreting a message can influence the next action of an agent as determined by the controller.

We now explain the interpretation and production modules in more detail. Since we assume that objects' perceptual features are categorised with given prototypes, we focus this explanation on how a shared lexicon can arise as part of the social symbol grounding process.

Interpretation

The language interpretation module (LIM) processes all messages that an agent receives. A message can consist of multiple words. For each word an agent receives, the LIM searches the lexicon (stored in the LTM) for entries that match the word. The lexicon is represented by two association matrices (Figure 3), one that maintains association scores $\sigma_{ij} \in \langle 0,1 \rangle$ and one that maintains a posteriori probabilities $P_{ij} = P(w_i|m_j)$ of finding word w_i, given meaning m_j. The association scores contain information about the association's effectiveness as evaluated through feedback. However, since we assume that feedback is not always provided, nor always accurate, the agents also maintain the co-occurrence probabilities allowing for cross-situational learning. The reason for using two types of scores is that earlier studies have revealed that using the probability type score is less efficient (read slower) if feedback is present, whereas using the association scores σ_{ij} does not work well for cross-situational learning (Vogt & Coumans, 2003).

When a hearer searches its lexicon, it selects the association matching the heard word and of which the association strength $strL_{ij}$ is highest. (If the word is not in the lexicon, the interaction fails and the word is adopted as explained later.) The association strength is a coupling between the two scores σ_{ij} and P_{ij}:

$$strL_{ij} = \sigma_{ij} + (1 - \sigma_{ij})P_{ij}. \tag{1}$$

	m_1	$\cdots$	m_N		m_1	$\cdots$	m_N
w_1	σ_{11}	$\cdots$	σ_{1N}	w_1	P_{11}	$\cdots$	P_{1N}
$\vdots$	$\vdots$	$\vdots$	$\vdots$	$\vdots$	$\vdots$	$\vdots$	$\vdots$
w_M	σ_{M1}	$\cdots$	σ_{MN}	w_M	P_{M1}	$\cdots$	P_{MN}

Figure 3. A simplified illustration of the lexicon. The lexicon consists of two matrices associating meanings m_j with words w_i. The left matrix stores association scores σ_{ij} and the right matrix stores co-occurrence probabilities P_{ij}.

This coupling assures that the association strength relies more on the association score σ_{ij} if it is high (i.e., it has been effective in previous interactions); otherwise $strL_{ij}$ relies more on the co-occurrence probability P_{ij}.

To establish joint attention, the speaker may have pointed to a target object o_t that relates to the message's meaning M_t, which is constructed by the speaker (s) as a subset of the target's category set CS_t^s (i.e., $M_t \subseteq CS_t^s$). Suppose m_j is the interpretation of one word (w_j) from the message. To estimate the outcome of this interpretation, the following steps are taken:

1. If an object is pointed to, the context Cxt is reduced to the hearer's category set CS_t^h of that target object. Now,
   (a) if $m_j \in CS_t^h$, the interpretation of word w_i is considered a *success*.
   (b) if $m_j \notin CS_t^h$, there are two possibilities:
      i. The association score $\sigma_{ij} > \Theta$ (where $\Theta = 0.8$ is a threshold), in which case it is assumed that the interpretation is correct, but the speaker got it wrong.
      ii. If $\sigma_{ij} \leq \Theta$, the interpretation is assumed to be the hearer's failure.
2. If no object is pointed to, and
   (a) $\sigma_{ij} > \Theta$, then the interpretation is considered a success. Otherwise,
   (b) the agent will — with some probability — either assume success or assume a hearer failure.

If the interpretation was considered a success for all words in a message, the controller adds it to the STM for further processing. Note that for step 2, the target relating to the interpreted meaning need not be in the hearer's context, so the agents can ground some knowledge about the environment without actually seeing it.

When the interpretation of all words has finished, the hearer may send a hardwired feedback signal to the speaker. This signal is sent with a probability proportional to the socialness gene and inversely proportional to their social bond.[4] This way, if the agent is social and does not know the speaker well, it is inclined to provide feedback, which should allow further learning. The feedback signals that can be sent are:

1. *Success* if the hearer considers the interpretation to be correct for all words.
2. *Speaker-error* if the hearer assumes the speaker to be wrong for at least one word.
3. *Interpretation-error* if there is a hearer failure for at least one word or when the hearer hears an unknown word.

Note that this feedback depends on the hearer's *estimation* of the game's outcome, but the hearer may be wrong as it has no means of verifying exactly what the

	m_1	m_2
w_1	0.8	0.2
w_2	0.1	0.7

	m_1	m_2	m_3
w_1	0.8	0.2	0.0
w_2	0.1	0.7	0.0
w_3	0.02	0.03	0.1

Figure 4. An illustration of the principle of contrast. Suppose the leftmost table shows the lexicon containing the association scores before acquiring the word w_3, which is heard in the context $Cxt=\{m_1,m_2,m_3\}$. Both w_3 and m_3 are added to the lexicon, where the association scores of w_3 with meanings m_1 and m_2 are inversely proportional to the highest association scores already existing for these meanings, and the association with m_3 is highest, since this meaning had no existing association.

speaker's meaning of a word is. This is different from the guessing games used in, for example, Steels et al. (2002), where the agents verify whether they refer to the same target.

If a success feedback signal was sent, the used association scores σ_{ij} for both agents are increased, while all competing association scores σ_{kl} ($k=i$ or $l=j$, but not both) are laterally inhibited. If an interpretation error signal was sent, both agents also lower the association scores of the interpretation. In case of a speaker error, only the speaker lowers the association score. In addition, in all cases the co-occurrence probabilities P_{ij} of each word with all meanings in the context Cxt (or $CS_t^{s,h}$) are adapted accordingly. (For more details on these adaptations, consult Divina & Vogt, 2006).

When interpretation is assumed to have failed or when a word is not in the lexicon, the LIM adds this word w_n to the lexicon in association with all categories in the Cxt (or CS_t^h in case the target was pointed to), provided the association does not already exists. The frequency counters of these associations are set to 1 and — to simulate the *principle of contrast* — the association scores σ_{nj} are initialised with:

$$\sigma_{nj} = (1 - \max_i(\sigma_{ij}))\sigma_0, \tag{2}$$

where $\max_i(\sigma_{ij})$ is the maximum association score that meaning m_j has with other words w_i, $i \neq n$ and $\sigma_0 = 0.1$ is a constant. This way, if the agent has already associated the meaning (or category) m_j with another word w_i, the agent is biased to prefer another meaning with this word (see Figure 4 for an example). It is important to note that since the agents do not share their visual fields, the hearer may not have seen the object relating to the word's meaning, so the new acquisitions may be wrong.

Production

When the LIM has finished processing, the control module will decide upon an action to take using all categories resulting from the categorisation and language interpretation as input. So, the information acquired through interpreting a message may influence this decision process.

Regardless of the action, the language production module (LPM) is started, because even if the action is not to talk, the LPM may nevertheless decide to communicate about something. This happens with a probability proportional to its socialness gene, provided the agent sees another agent. If the agent received an 'interpretation error' message, the LPM always decides to communicate about the object it communicated about before, provided the object is still in the context, but now the probability that the message is accompanied by a pointing gesture is increased. If no interpretation error was received and the agent has decided to communicate, a meaning is selected as follows.

First, a task complexity C_t is chosen. The task complexity is a value that indicates how many words the message will contain. C_t is a value between 1 and 5 such that the agent will tend to speak shorter sentences to younger agents and longer sentences to older agents. The rationale is that shorter sentences are easier to interpret by less skilled language users than longer sentences. Second, one target object is selected randomly from the objects in the speaker's visual field and the message's meaning M_t is formed from selecting C_t arbitrary categories from the category set CS_t^s relating to this target.

For each category, the LPM searches its lexicon for associations whose meaning matches the category and for which the association strength $strL_{ij}$ (Eq. 1) is highest. The associated word is then appended to the message. If a category has no entry in the lexicon yet, a new word is created as a random string and the new association is added to the lexicon. It is important to realise that agents are 'born' with an empty lexicon.

Once a message is thus constructed, the LPM decides, with a probability proportional to its social bias, whether the agent will point to an object that directly relates to the message's meaning. So, the more social the agent is, the more likely the speaker is to provide its audience with hints as to what it is referring to. This can, thus, be seen as a form of affective interaction as part of external symbol grounding (Cowley, 2006).

Experimental results

A number of experiments were done with the above model to investigate the effects of particular aspects of the learning mechanisms such as feedback, the principle of contrast, pointing and cross-situational learning. To keep our focus on these aspects, we switched off all evolutionary learning and individual learning mechanisms.

All experiments were run for 36,500 time steps, which is slightly longer than an agent's maximum lifespan. Agents were able to reproduce after they lived for 3,650 time steps, so the population size remained constant at the initial size of 100 during the first 3,650 time steps. Thereafter the population size increased slightly in all simulations, but kept fluctuating on average around 110 agents. This is because from that moment, many agents tended to die from their loss of energy expended during reproduction (offspring receives 50% of their parents' energy). Throughout all simulations, about 20% of the population initiated a language game each time step, so during one simulation — assuming an average population size of 110 agents — about 739,200 messages were sent. The agents tend to talk only in small groups because of their spatial distribution. On average, 44% of all language games were accompanied by a pointing gesture, in 12% of all games a feedback singal was sent, and in 48% of all games neither pointing nor feedback was used.

The effectiveness of the language evolution was monitored with *communicative accuracy* (or *accuracy* for short). Accuracy was measured at every 30 time steps by dividing the total number of *successful* language games by the total number of language games played during that period. A language game is determined successful if the hearer interpreted the speaker's expression with the exact intended meaning (not the intended referent). We prefer to use the term communicative accuracy rather than, for example, communicative success, because the interpretations need to yield intended meanings. Communicative success would be used if success was evaluated based on identifying the intended referent irrespective of the meaning representation. Since there is a one-to-one relation between meaning and referent in the current setting, communicative accuracy implies communicative success. For statistical purposes, all results we present are averages of 10 different trials of each setting with different random seeds.

In all simulations, the agents were given 6 feature channels (out of a maximum of 10) with which to detect 5 different types of objects having a total of 26 different perceptual features.[5] This means that each object (except agents) was perceived with 5 different perceptual features (colour, shape, characteristics, direction and distance); agents were perceived with the additional feature of sex (either male or female). So, if during a language game an object was pointed to, the a priori chance of communicative accuracy is 1/5 (or 1/6). If no object was pointed to, the a priori chance of accuracy was between 1/5 and 1/24 (or between 1/6 and 1/26), depending on the number of objects in the context.

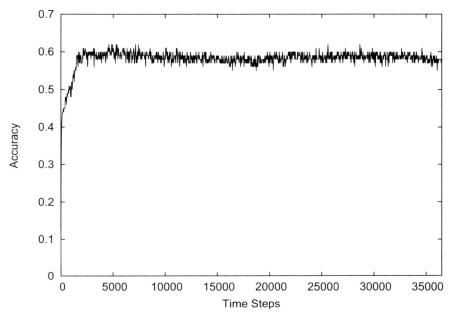

Figure 5. This figure shows the evolution of accuracy over time in the first experiment.

A first experiment

A first experiment was carried out with the model as described in the previous section. Figure 5 shows the evolution of accuracy during this experiment. Accuracy increased rapidly during the first 2,000 time steps to a value around 0.6. From then on, accuracy remained more or less stable. Although accuracy did not reach a high level (we discuss the reason why in the Discussion section), the system performed better than expected.

   Although the lexicons of individual agents increased to up to an average of 250 words, they tended to use far fewer words as some were heard perhaps only once from an occasional contact with another agent. On average, the number of words used by the whole population during the final 1,000 time steps was 50. This means that — on average — only two different words were used by the population to express a meaning. This is surprising, since during their lifetime, each agent does not meet every other agent, nor are they likely to communicate with half of the population frequently enough to align their lexicons through direct communication. Hence, the language seems to have diffused over the population. However, given that individual lexicons contain an average of 250 words, there also may be considerable language change, though many of these words could come from sporadic inventions by young agents and their use across the populations.

Excluding learning mechanisms

In the second series of simulations, we varied the use of particular learning mechanisms by running experiments in which we switched off one of the following learning mechanisms:

No feedback. In these experiments, the agents did not provide feedback signals. As a result, the association scores σ_{ij} were never adapted, though their initial scores were still initialised following Eq. (2).

No principle of contrast. In these simulations, the principle of contrast was switched off (i.e., Eq. (2) was not used) and each novel association was initialised with the same association score σ_0.

No pointing. In this setting, no message was accompanied by a pointing gesture, so each context size was somewhere between 6 and 26, depending on the number of objects in the hearer's visual field.

No cross-situational learning. In these simulations, the co-occurrence probabilities P_{ij} were never updated. So $strL_{ij} = \sigma_{ij}$, which is only updated through feedback and the principle of contrast.

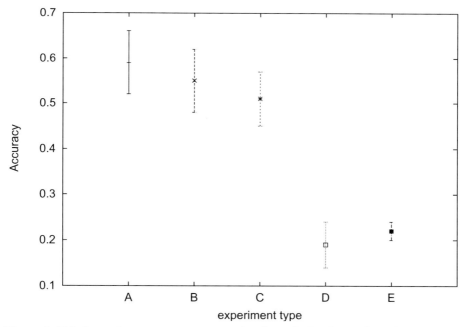

Figure 6. This figure shows accuracy measured at the end of each set of simulations for (A) the standard model and those that exclude either (B) feedback, (C) principle of contrast, (D) pointing or (E) cross-situational learning. Error bars indicate the standard deviations across different runs.

Figure 6 shows the results of his experiment as measured at the end of each set of simulations. For comparison, the results of the standard model used in the previous section are included. The graph shows that feedback and the principle of contrast had little influence on the level of accuracy. A Wilcoxon rank sum test has shown that the effect of removing the principle of contrast was more significant ($p = 0.0177$) than that of removing feedback ($p = 0.0526$). We introduced feedback, because we believed that this would improve learning enough to allow for damping of synonymy when adapting the association scores; a mechanism that was shown to be important in cross-situational learning in large populations (De Beule et al., 2006). We introduced the principle of contrast as an extra bias against synonymy, and although the effect is small, it appears significant.

Pointing and cross-situational learning, however, had a large impact. Pointing, of course, is used to reduce referential indeterminacy to the number of perceptual features. Cross-situational learning then refines the learning of word-meanings. Note that removing cross-situational learning does not reduce the model to the guessing game, because the infrequent updates of the association scores are based on unreliable feedback.

Discussion

In this paper we study social symbol grounding in a multi-agent simulation of a relatively complex world. This study focuses on how a shared system of grounded symbols can evolve based on a model that combines learning mechanisms such as feedback, the principle of contrast, joint attention (through pointing) and cross-situational learning. In this section, we discuss the experimental results, their implications and some future work.

We have argued that the social symbol grounding problem is probably harder than the physical symbol grounding problem (which is symbol grounding for an individual), because of the referential indeterminacy problem (Quine, 1960) that arises with the need for making conventions. The experiments have shown that to acquire and understand the verbal communication of other individuals, participants of language games benefit from engaging in triadic behaviours such as joint attention, because it reduces referential indeterminacy from all possible meanings in the context to all possible meanings relating to the attended object.

This means that the social activity of engaging in joint attention is crucial for this model. It is hard to generalise this finding to human societies, but since the point at which infants start to use joint attention activities coincides with the start of language use (Tomasello, 1999), joint attention skills seem crucial for social symbol grounding in general.

As mentioned before, pointing is not sufficient to eliminate all referential indeterminacy, because an object has a number of perceptual features and — in this model — a word refers to a single perceptual feature. (As the gavagai example illustrates, this holds in general.) To deal with the remaining uncertainty of a word's meaning, cross-situational learning could be a crucial mechanism, as this, too, has an significant impact on the success of evolving a shared lexicon in the model.

Although it has been shown mathematically that cross-situational learning can work if the context size is relatively large (K. Smith et al., 2006), for large populations it has been shown that evolving a coherent lexicon is quite hard, even for small context sizes (Vogt & Coumans, 2003). It must therefore be beneficial for cross-situational learning if agents engage in joint attention activities as this reduces the effective context size.

Feedback and the principle of contrast have little influence in this model, but it is even harder to validate these findings in general, because that would require more comparative experiments using more controlled environments. Regarding feedback, the small effect is most likely due to the fact that feedback does not make use of a mechanism to evaluate the success of a language game reliably. Agents only assume success if the association strength reaches a certain threshold. Feedback based on the evaluation of success, using explicit meaning transfer or verifying whether both agents have identified the same referent, has proven to be very effective (Steels et al., 2002; Vogt & Coumans, 2003). Future extensions of this model should therefore consider a means to evaluate successful interpretation more reliably.

It is likely that the contrast implemented (i.e., the differences between initial association scores) is too small, so that it only has an effect for a brief period. To prolong that period, we need to enlarge the initial differences by using a larger initial score σ_0 in Eq. (2).

Although much better than chance, the level of accuracy reached in the experiments (±60%) is far from optimal. It is hard to assess exactly why this is the case, but we can identify at least two reasons why grounding a shared lexicon is hard. First, a word does not always co-occur in a context containing its meaning, because the hearer may not have seen the target object intended by the speaker. The reason for this is that the speaker and hearer cannot be at the same location at the same time (see Figure 7). Furthermore, the speaker does not check the hearer's orientation, so both agents may have completely different visual fields. This is no problem if the hearer already acquired the word-meaning mapping reliably, but it is harmful for learning. Previous tests have shown that when agents use explicit meaning transfer (i.e., the exact meaning is provided to the hearer), accuracy increases to 97% (Divina & Vogt, 2006).

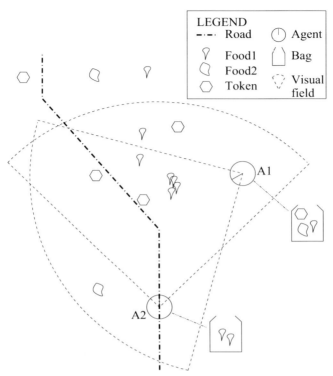

Figure 7. A possible situation for a language game. The two agents, A1 and A2 are inside each other's visual field (dashed arcs), but they do not share a context (i.e., visual field). As a result, the hearer may not have seen the intended target. Note that this is a near ideal situation; many situations will have more dissimilar contexts.

Second, because agents develop their own lexicon independently and from scratch, different agents may create different words to express the same meanings, so the maximum number of words created in a lexicon increases with the population. The task for the population is then to reduce the number of words being used. Such a reduction works well if the agents have a strong form of explicit meaning transfer, but it becomes harder if there is no strict one-to-one bias between words and meanings. We hope to improve accuracy in the future by incorporating the one-to-one bias model introduced by De Beule et al. (2006).

The extent to which accuracy can be improved remains to be seen. We are currently trying to improve the model by investigating the effect of changing parameter settings and modifying methods. We have described a different evaluation mechanism for the feedback process, changing the initial association score for improving the principle of contrast and the model of De Beule et al. However, the effectiveness of the social symbol grounding process is not only realised by the learning mechanisms and the quality of non-verbal interactions, but also by environmental constraints and population dynamics.

Regarding the former, we described the problems in sharing the context. More sophisticated methods for checking the 'focus' of attention might be developed to improve setting a common ground. This way, an agent might take into consideration what the other agent sees (and perhaps even knows). Hence, they might need something like a Theory of Mind (Premack & Woodruff, 1978). In addition, to allow better generalisations toward human societies, we need to perform comparative experiments using other platforms, such as the Talking Heads simulator (Vogt, 2005).

Regarding the population dynamic, the world is a spatial environment and agents are distributed over the entire world, though clusters (of agents and language) may emerge in the population.[6] Since agents move around, they will encounter new agents who speak another language, which has a negative effect on accuracy. The rate of population flow, their distribution in the world and the speed with which they can move will influence accuracy. Interestingly, though, language contact also seems to allow language diffusion (unless the language changes rapidly), which could explain how large language communities form. Further studies should investigate more thoroughly what exactly is happening.

In future experiments, we plan to extend the simulations, such that they are integrated with evolutionary, individual and social learning. Regarding the latter, we intend to extend the model with the social learning of skills where skills are transmitted using language. To accomplish this, the agents will communicate parts of their decision process as evaluated by their controller. As mentioned, the controller is a decision Q-tree that can be adapted using reinforcement learning (Gilbert et al., 2006). The idea is that agents adapt their DQTs by inserting new nodes based on the heard decision process of other agents, thus allowing them to align parts of their DQTs with those of others. This way, communicated meanings become more meaningful regarding the agents' survival, therefore surmounting true (social) symbol grounding (Ziemke & Sharkey, 2001)

Conclusions

In this paper we explore how the social symbol grounding problem can be investigated using large scale multi-agent systems to evolve social and other behavioural skills to survive in a complex environment over extended periods of time. In particular, we investigate a novel hybrid model of language learning that involves joint attention, feedback, cross-situational learning and the principle of contrast.

The experiments show that — although the system does not work optimally — levels of communicative accuracy better than chance evolve quite rapidly in this system. In addition, they show that accuracy is mainly achieved by the joint attention and cross-situational learning mechanisms and that feedback and the principle of contrast do not contribute much. However, further experiments using different parameter settings, platforms and learning mechanisms are required to generalise these findings.

The research to be carried out with the New Ties platform has only just started and, to increase the number of related studies, the New Ties platform has been made publicly available.[7] We encourage other researchers to use this platform — which we think allows the study of symbol grounding in a social context — and challenges will be published to set out benchmark experiments. One way to extend the current model is to allow populations using language to learn behavioural skills from each other. This would take social symbol grounding to a higher level.

Acknowledgements

This research and the New Ties project is supported by an EC FET grant under contract 003752. We thank all members the New Ties project for their invaluable contributions. Opinions and errors in this manuscript are the authors' responsibility, they do not necessarily reflect those of the EC or other New Ties members. Paul Vogt is supported by a VENI grant awarded by the Netherlands Organisation for Scientific Research (NWO). Special thanks to Andrew Smith and three anonymous reviewers for their invaluable comments on earlier versions of this manuscript.

Notes

1. New Ties stands for New Emerging World models Through Individual, Evolutionary and Social learning. See http://www.new-ties.org.

2. Note that Peirce used a different terminology than that adopted here. He used *object, interpretant* and *representamen* to denote what we call *referent, meaning* and *form*, respectively. The adopted terminology is more common in modern cognitive science.

3. The current state of the project is that most parts have been implemented and tested, and preliminary experiments are being carried out.

4. The social bond is based on the frequency with which two agents have interacted with each other.

5. In Divina and Vogt (2006) we have investigated the effect of the number of feature channels on the level of accuracy. The results have shown that, if the agents perceive up to 6 features, accuracy evolves to a lower level and then more or less stabilises, because additional features, such as age, are not always observable for some objects.

6. Methods are being developed to discover clusters in the population regarding similarities in language and controllers.

7. http://www.new-ties.org.

References

Akhtar, N., & Montague, L. (1999). Early lexical acquisition: The role of cross-situational learning. *First Language, 19*, 347–358.

Bloom, P. (2000). *How children learn the meanings of words.* Cambridge, MA. and London, UK.: The MIT Press.

Cangelosi, A. (2001). Evolution of communication and language using signals, symbols and words. *IEEE Transactions of Evolutionary Computation, 5*, 93–101.

Cangelosi, A. (2006). The grounding and sharing of symbols. *Pragmatics and Cognition, 14*, 275–285.

Cangelosi, A., & Parisi, D. (Eds.). (2002). *Simulating the evolution of language.* London: Springer.

Chouinard, M. M., & Clark, E. V. (2003). Adult reformulations of child errors as negative evidence. *Journal of Child Language, 30(3)*, 637–669.

Clark, E. V. (1993). *The lexicon in acquisition.* Cambridge University Press.

Cowley, S. J. (2006). Distributed language: biomechanics, functions and the origins of talk. In C. Lyon, C. Nehaniv, & A. Cangelosi (Eds.), *Emergence and evolution of linguistic communication.* Springer.

De Beule, J., De Vylder, B., & Belpaeme, T. (2006). A cross-situational learning algorithm for damping homonymy in the guessing game. In L. Rocha, L. Yaeger, M. Bedau, D. Floreano, R. Goldstone, & A. Vespignani (Eds.), *ALIFE X. Tenth international conference on the simulation and synthesis of living systems.* Cambridge, MA: MIT Press.

Divina, F., & Vogt, P. (2006). A hybrid model for learning word-meaning mappings. In P. Vogt, Y. Sugita, E. Tuci, & C. Nehaniv (Eds.), *Symbol grounding and beyond.* Springer.

Epstein, J. M., & Axtell, R. (1996). *Growing artificial societies: social science from the bottom up.* Cambridge, MA.: MIT Press.

Gärdenfors, P. (2000). *Conceptual spaces.* Bradford Books, MIT Press.

Gilbert, N., Besten, M. den, Bontovics, A., Craenen, B., Divina, F., Eiben, A., et al. (2006). Emerging artificial societies through learning. *Journal of Artificial Societies and Social Simulation, 9(2).*

Harnad, S. (1990). The symbol grounding problem. *Physica D, 42*, 335–346.

Houston-Price, C., Plunkett, K., & Harris, P. (2005). 'Word-learning wizardry' at 1;6. *Journal of Child Language, 32*, 175–190.

Kirby, S., & Hurford, J. R. (2002). The emergence of linguistic structure: An overview of the iterated learning model. In A. Cangelosi & D. Parisi (Eds.), *Simulating the evolution of language* (p. 121–148). London: Springer.

Ogden, C. K., & Richards, I. A. (1923). *The meaning of meaning: A study of the influence of language upon thought and of the science of symbolism.* London: Routledge & Kegan Paul Ltd.

Oliphant, M., & Batali, J. (1997). Learning and the emergence of coordinated communication. *Center for Research on Language Newsletter, 11(1).*

Peirce, C. S. (1931–1958). *Collected papers* (Vol. I-VIII). Cambridge Ma.: Harvard University Press.

Premack, D., & Woodruff, G. (1978). Does the chimpanzee have a theory of mind? *Behavioral and Brain Sciences, 1(4)*, 515–526.

Quine, W. V. O. (1960). *Word and object.* Cambridge University Press.

Roy, D. (2005). Semiotic schemas: A framework for grounding language in action and perception. *Artificial Intelligence, 167*, 170–205.

Siskind, J. M. (1996). A computational study of cross-situational techniques for learning word-to-meaning mappings. *Cognition, 61*, 39–91.

aSmith, A. D. M. (2005). Mutual exclusivity: Communicative success despite conceptual divergence. In M. Tallerman (Ed.), *Language origins: perspectives on evolution* (pp. 372–388). Oxford: Oxford University Press.

Smith, K., Smith, A., Blythe, R., & Vogt, P. (2006). Cross-situational learning: a mathematical approach. In P. Vogt, Y. Sugita, E. Tuci, & C. Nehaniv (Eds.), *Symbol grounding and beyond.* Springer.

Steels, L. (1997). The synthetic modeling of language origins. *Evolution of Communication, 1(1)*, 1–34.

Steels, L., & Belpaeme, T. (2005). Coordinating perceptually grounded categories through language: A case study for colour. *Behavioral and Brain Sciences, 28*, 469–529.

Steels, L., Kaplan, F., McIntyre, A., & Van Looveren, J. (2002). Crucial factors in the origins of word-meaning. In A. Wray (Ed.), *The transition to language.* Oxford, UK: Oxford University Press.

Tomasello, M. (1999). *The cultural origins of human cognition.* Harvard University Press.

Vogt, P. (2000). Bootstrapping grounded symbols by minimal autonomous robots. *Evolution of Communication, 4(1)*, 89–118.

Vogt, P. (2002). The physical symbol grounding problem. *Cognitive Systems Research, 3(3)*, 429–457.

Vogt, P. (2005). The emergence of compositional structures in perceptually grounded language games. *Artificial Intelligence, 167(1–2)*, 206–242.

Vogt, P. (2006). Language evolution and robotics: Issues in symbol grounding and language acquisition. In A. Loula, R. Gudwin, & J. Queiroz (Eds.), *Artificial cognition systems.* Idea Group.

Vogt, P., & Coumans, H. (2003). Investigating social interaction strategies for bootstrapping lexicon development. *Journal for Artificial Societies and Social Simulation, 6(1).* (http://jasss.soc.surrey.ac.uk)

Ziemke, T., & Sharkey, N. E. (2001). A stroll through the worlds of robots and animals: Applying Jakob von Uexküll's theory of meaning to adaptive robots and artificial life. *Semiotica, 134(1–4)*, 701–746.

How many words can my robot learn?

An approach and experiments with one-class learning

Luís Seabra Lopes and Aneesh Chauhan
Universidade de Aveiro, Portugal

This paper addresses word learning for human–robot interaction. The focus is on making a robotic agent aware of its surroundings, by having it learn the names of the objects it can find. The human user, acting as instructor, can help the robotic agent ground the words used to refer to those objects. A lifelong learning system, based on one-class learning, was developed (OCLL). This system is incremental and evolves with the presentation of any new word, which acts as a class to the robot, relying on instructor feedback. A novel experimental evaluation methodology, that takes into account the open-ended nature of word learning, is proposed and applied. This methodology is based on the realization that a robot's vocabulary will be limited by its discriminatory capacity which, in turn, depends on its sensors and perceptual capabilities. The results indicate that the robot's representations are capable of incrementally evolving by correcting class descriptions, based on instructor feedback to classification results. In successive experiments, it was possible for the robot to learn between 6 and 12 names of real-world office objects. Although these results are comparable to those obtained by other authors, there is a need to scale-up. The limitations of the method are discussed and potential directions for improvement are pointed out.

Keywords: human–robot interaction, external symbol grounding, word learning, one-class learning, experimental methodologies

Introduction

The robotics community is increasingly involved in designing and developing user-friendly robots, that is, robots that are flexible, adaptable and easy to command and instruct (Breazeal & Scassellati, 2000; Chatila, 2004; Fong, Nourbakhsh & Dautenhahn, 2003; Seabra Lopes & Connell, 2001b). A user-friendly robot must be prepared to adapt to the user. This adaptation includes the capacity to take a high-level description of the assigned task and carry out the necessary reasoning steps to determine exactly what must be done. Reasoning capabilities such as action sequence planning or logical inference are, by definition, based on manipulating symbolic representations.

User-friendliness also includes understanding and using the communication modalities of the human user. Spoken language is probably the most powerful communication modality. It can reduce the problem of assigning a task to the robot to a simple sentence, and it can also play a major role in teaching the robot new facts and behaviors. There is, therefore, a trend to develop robots with spoken language capabilities (Levinson, Squire, Lin & McClain, 2005; Seabra Lopes, 2002; Seabra Lopes, Teixeira, Quinderé & Rodrigues, 2005; Steels & Kaplan, 2002; see also several reports in Seabra Lopes & Connell, 2001a).

This paper addresses word learning for human–robot interaction. The learning paradigm of choice for this work is one-class learning. An incremental learning system based on Support Vector Data Description (Tax, 2001) was developed to support the grounding of word meanings. Given the open-ended nature of word learning, this system is designed to support the concurrent/opportunistic learning of an arbitrary number of classes/words. Through mechanisms of shared attention and corrective feedback, a human user, acting as an instructor, can help the robot ground the words used to refer to real-world office objects that it finds in its environment. A novel experimental evaluation methodology is proposed for word learning. This methodology took two main considerations into account. On the one hand, word learning is an open-ended domain. On the other hand, an agent's vocabulary will be limited by its discriminatory capacity which, in turn, depends on its sensors and perceptual capabilities. This methodology can be useful for comparing the word learning capabilities of different agents and for assessing research progress on scaling-up to larger vocabularies.

Situating the problem

Symbol and language grounding

Both reasoning and language processing involve the manipulation of symbols. By *symbol* we mean a pattern that represents some entity in the world by association, resemblance or convention. Association and resemblance arise from perceptual, sensorimotor and functional aspects while convention is socially or culturally established.

The advent of computers encouraged people to start developing "intelligent" artifacts, including artifacts with human-level intelligence (Turing, 1950). As reasoning and language are key components of intelligence, the first few decades of research on artificial intelligence (AI) focused on first-order logic, semantic networks, logical inference, search techniques and natural language processing. Symbol systems in AI were theorized by Simon and Newell in successive publications since the 1970s, and became the dominant model of the mind in cognitive science (see the survey and critical analysis of Anderson & Perlis, 2002).

These symbolic representations were amodal in the sense that they had no obvious correspondence or resemblance to their referents (Barsalou, 1999). As aspects related to perception and sensorimotor control were largely overlooked, establishing the connection between symbols and their referents remained an open issue. The problem of making the semantic interpretation of a formal symbol system intrinsic to that system was called "the symbol grounding problem" (Harnad, 1990). Eventually, the limitations of classical symbolic AI led to a vigorous reaction, generally known as "situated" or "embodied" AI, and, in particular, to the "intelligence without representation" views of Brooks (1991).

In the meantime, the resurgence of connectionism led various authors to propose hybrid symbolic/connectionist approaches. In particular, Harnad (1990) proposed a hybrid approach to the "symbol grounding problem," which consists of grounding bottom-up symbolic representations in iconic representations (sensory projections of objects) and categorical representations (learned or innate connectionist functions capable of extracting invariant features from sensory projections). Elementary symbols are the names of these categories. More complex representations are obtained by aggregating elementary symbols.

The increasing concern with perception and sensorimotor control, both in the AI and robotics communities, was paralleled in cognitive science. Barsalou (1999) develops a theory on "perceptual symbol systems," which takes up the classical (perceptual) view of cognition. A "perceptual symbol" is viewed as an unconscious neural representation that represents some component of perceptual experience. Related perceptual symbols become organized into a kind of category or concept, called a simulator. The simulator is able to produce limitless simulations (conscious mental images of members of the category) even in the absence of specific perceptual experience. Simulators can be aggregated in frames to produce simulators for more complex categories. Linguistic symbols are viewed as perceptual symbols for spoken or written words. As linguistic simulators develop, they become associated with the simulators of the entities to which they refer.

Taking a broader perspective, Clark (1997) sees control of embodied action as an emergent property of a distributed system composed of brain, body and environment. However, Clark rejects radical anti-representationalist approaches and accepts the need for representations geared to specific sensorimotor needs. He also emphasizes the importance of external scaffolding, that is, the support provided to thought by the environment and by public language.

A distributed view on language origins, evolution and acquisition is emerging in linguistics. This trend emphasizes that language is a cultural product, perpetually open-ended and incomplete, ambiguous to some extent and, therefore, not a code (Love, 2004). The study of language origins and evolution has been performed using multi-robot models, with the Talking Heads experiments as a notable example (Steels, 2001). Steels and Kaplan (2002) have reported a related robotic approach to language acquisition. Given that language acquisition and evolution, both in human and artificial agents, involve not only internal, but also cultural, social and affective processes, the underlying mechanism has been called "external symbol grounding" (Cowley, 2007a).

The symbol grounding problem was originally formulated as a problem of formal symbol systems and classical AI (Harnad, 1990). However, most research on symbol grounding has been taking place within cognitive science, usually with a strong cognitive modeling flavor and, therefore, with concerns for psychological plausibility (Cangelosi, 2005). However, it is becoming necessary to study symbol and language grounding from an engineering perspective, that is, having in mind the development of machines with reasoning and language skills suitable for practical applications. The main criterion here is no longer the psychological plausibility of the approaches but their utility. This is consistent with a modern view of AI, which no longer concentrates on solving problems by simulating human intelligence, but rather on developing practically useful systems with the most suitable approaches.

Word learning

This paper addresses word learning with a motivation coming from the area of human–robot interaction. Word learning is a basic language acquisition task and, therefore, relies on external symbol grounding mechanisms. For artificial agents, the problem is designing suitable mechanisms for this. Cognitive models and robotic prototypes have been developed for the acquisition of a series of words or labels for naming certain categories of objects. The next paragraphs provide an overview of some of the main published models and prototypes.

Harnad, Hanson, and Lubin (1991, 1995) study categorical perception effects (within-category compression and between-category expansion) with a three-layer feed-forward network. The work involved the sorting of lines into three categories ("short," "middle," "long"). Plunkett and collaborators (Plunkett, Sinha, Moller

& Strandsby, 1992; Plunkett & Sinha, 1992) use a dual-route connectionist architecture with auto-associative learning for studying language production and understanding. Retinal and verbal information were present in both input and output layers, and the network had two hidden layers. After training, the network could be used both for language generation (object category name, given visual perception) and understanding (object visualization given the name). Sales and Evans (1995) used a dual-route architecture based on "weightless artificial neurons." They claim that their system can easily acquire 50 grounded nouns, although the demonstration is limited to three object categories ("apple," "jar" and "cup").

Roy and Pentland (2002) present a system that learns to segment words out of continuous speech from a caregiver while associating these words with co-occurring visual categories. The implementation assumes that caregivers tend to repeat words referring to salient objects in the environment. Therefore, the system searches for recurring words in similar visual contexts. Two-dimensional histograms for multiple views for representing each object and a chi-squared distance metric were used for comparing objects. Word meanings for seven object classes were learned (e.g., a few toy animals, a ball.)

Steels and Kaplan (2002, see also Steels, 2001) use the notion of "language game" to develop a social learning framework through which an AIBO robot can learn its first words with human mediation. The mediator, as a teacher, points to objects and provides their names. The robot uses color histograms and an instance-based learning method to learn word meanings. The mediator can also ask questions and provide feedback on the robot's answers. Names were learned for three objects: "Poo-Chi," "Red Ball" and "Smiley." While Harnad (1990) argued for bottom-up grounding of symbolic representations into categories, Steels and Kaplan show, with concrete robotic experiments, that unsupervised category formation may produce categories that are completely unrelated to the categories that are needed for grounding the words of the used language. They therefore conclude that social interaction must be used to help the learner focus on what needs to be learned. This is in line with previous linguistic and philosophical theories, including the Sapir-Whorf thesis (Talmy, 2000; for a related recent study, see Yoshida & Smith, 2005).

Levinson et al. (2005) describe a robot that learns to associate meanings using a cascade of hidden Markov models. After about 30 minutes of training, the robot is able to associate linguistic expressions with four objects: a green ball, a red ball, a toy dog and a toy cat. The linguistic expressions designate two abstract categories ("animal" and "ball") and four concrete categories ("green ball," "red ball," "dog" and "cat").

Yu (2005) studies, through a computational model, the interaction between lexical acquisition and object categorization. In a pre-linguistic phase, shape (histograms), color and texture (Gabor filters) information from vision is used to ground word meanings. After the application of PCA, Gaussian mixtures are used to cluster the category description. In a later phase, linguistic labels are used as an additional teaching signal that enhances object categorization. A total of 12 object categories (pictures of animals in a book for small children) was used for experiments.

Greco, Riga, and Cangelosi (2003) study grounding transfer, that is, the process of building composed symbolic representations from grounded elementary symbols, as originally proposed by Harnad (1990). They present two simulations based on connectionist architectures: one with four shape categories, four texture categories and four composed categories, and the other with three color categories, three shape categories and nine composed categories.

This survey includes quite different approaches, at all levels (e.g., embodiment, teaching/mediation, complexity of the named objects, feature extraction, learning method, number of training examples, learning time.). Nevertheless, they all seem to be limited in the number of classes or categories that can be learned (this number varies between 3 and 12 in the cited works). This limitation seems also to affect incremental/lifelong learning systems not specifically developed for word learning or symbol grounding. That is the case for Learn++ (Polikar, Udpa, Udpa & Honavar, 2001) and EBNN (Thrun, 1996). Steels and Kaplan (2002) and Cangelosi (2005) have already pointed out the need for scaling up the number of acquired categories for symbol/language grounding.

As can be seen from the survey, researchers have focused on naming visually observable concrete objects. This will also be the focus of the present paper. Interestingly, in the earliest moments of child language development, most of the vocabulary consists of common nouns that name concrete objects in the child's environment, such as food, toys and clothes. The rest includes routine social words, proper nouns, animal sounds, and almost no verbs or function words. The over-representation of common nouns (and corresponding under-representation of verbs) can be observed until the third birthday. Gillette, Gleitman, Gleitman and Lederer (1999) show that the more imageable or concrete the referent of a word is, the easier it is to learn. So concrete nouns are easier to learn than most verbs, but "observable" verbs can be easier to learn than abstract nouns. In learning words, children show several systematic attentional biases. For concrete solid objects, there is a bias towards generalizing object names to other instances based on shape (Gershhoff-Stowe & Smith, 2004; Samuelson & Smith, 2005; Smith & Samuelson, 2006). Concerning developmental evolution, vocabulary starts with about 10 words around the age of one, increases to about 300 words in the second year and continues increasing steadily until adolescence (Bates, Thal, Finlay & Clancy, 2002; Crystal, 1987). The average vocabulary for adults is in the order of several tens of thousands. Early categories associated to words are often not consistent with the categories of adults. It has been observed that, in later lexical development (ages of 5 to 14), categories are gradually reorganized to converge to the categories of adults (Ameel, Malt & Storms, 2006).

Learning requirements

Language grounding is highly dependent on the techniques and methods being used for learning. Learning a human language will require the participation of the human user as teacher or mediator (Seabra Lopes & Wang, 2002; Steels & Kaplan, 2002).

A learning system in a robot should support long-term learning and adaptation, as is common in animals and, particularly, in humans. For that purpose, the learning system should exhibit several basic properties (Seabra Lopes & Wang, 2002), namely:

- *Supervised* — to include the human instructor in the learning process. This is an essential property for supporting the external/social component of symbol grounding.
- *On-line* — so that learning takes place while the agent is running.
- *Opportunistic* — the system must be prepared to accept a new example when it is observed or becomes available, rather than at pre-defined times or according to a pre-defined training schedule. This is another essential property for complying with the dynamics underlying external grounding.
- *Incremental* — it is able to adjust the learned descriptions when a new example is observed.
- *Concurrent* — it is able to handle multiple learning problems at the same time.
- *Meta-learning* — it is able to determine which learning parameters are more promising for different problems, ensuring each problem is handled efficiently.

With respect to the specific learning technique or paradigm, symbol grounding involves finding the invariant perceptual properties of the objects or categories to which symbols refer (Barsalou, 1999; Harnad, 1990). This suggests that learning of symbol meanings should be (predominantly) based on positive examples. Additionally, it should be noted that it is not easy to provide counter-examples in open-ended domains like word learning. Learning from positive examples is the basis for the one-class learning paradigm (Japkowicz, 1999; Tax, 2001), which was adopted for the work described below, and in some previous work (Wang & Seabra Lopes, 2004).

Architecture

The whole system comprises two main components (Figure 1), namely the artificial agent (for historical reasons here called the Student) and its World (including the human Instructor). The agent architecture itself consists of a perception system, an internal lifelong learning and classification system (OCLL) and a limited action system. At present, the action system abilities are limited to reporting the classification results back to the Instructor. Since the current agent perceives and acts on the physical world, it will also be referred to as a robot.

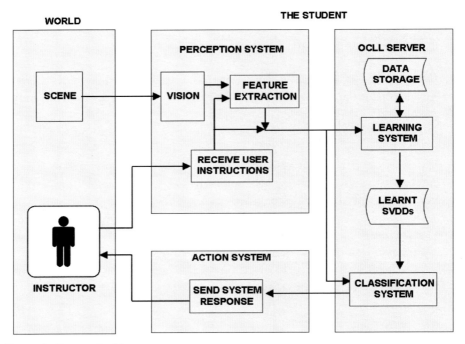

Figure 1. System Architecture

Instructor and the world

The world includes the user, a visually observable area and real-world objects (e.g., pen, stapler, mobile, mouse) whose names the instructor may wish to teach. The user, who is typically not visible to the robot, will act as instructor or mediator. As instructor, he or she has the role of communicating with the robot. Using a simple interface, the instructor can select (by mouse-clicking) any object from the robot's visible scene, thereby enabling shared attention. Then, the instructor can perform the following actions:

- Teach the object's class name for learning
- Ask the class name of the object, which the robot will determine based on previously learned knowledge
- If the class returned in the previous case is wrong, the instructor can send a correction.

The student

The student robot currently is a computer with an attached camera.[1] The computer runs the visual perception and learning/classification software as well as the communication interface for the instructor. The tasks of the perception system include capturing images from the camera, receiving instructions from the user (sending objects for either learning or classification) and extracting object features from images (Figure 1).

Once the user points the mouse to the desired object in the image, an edge-based counterpart of the whole image is generated.[2] From this edges image, the boundary of the object is extracted taking into account the user-pointed position.[3]

The boundary image contains all pixels located at the boundary edges of the object. Figure 2 illustrates the stated stages of pre-processing to extract the boundary image of the object class *Stapler*. At this point, the instructor can check whether the extracted boundary image adequately represents the object and decide whether to use it for learning or classification.

Objects should be described to the learning algorithm in terms of a small set of informative features. A small number of features will shorten the running time for the learning algorithm. Information content of the features will determine the learning performance. For visual object recognition in an artificial/robotic system, it seems crucial that features capture the object's shape. As mentioned earlier, children show a strong attentional bias towards shape when learning names of artifacts. Moreover, shape should be captured independently of position and orientation in the scene.

Figure 2. Image pre-processing stages in extracting the boundary of the object *Stapler* from the original image.
(*Left: the original scene; center: the edges image; right: the boundary image of Stapler*)

To meet these requirements, a feature extraction strategy was devised that captures the variation of the distance of boundary pixels to the center of the object. For this purpose, the smallest circle enclosing the object is divided into 36 sections of 10°. Each section i contains a number of boundary pixels with angle θ_i, such that $10 \times (i-1) \leq \theta_i < 10 \times i$. The average distance of these pixels to the center of the circle, a radius R_i, is computed. Based on the R_i values, the following features are then computed:

- Radius average, R — the average of all R_i.
- Radius standard deviation, S — again computed over all R_i.
- Normalized radii, r_i — this is a vector containing the normalization of all R_i values with respect to the average radius R, but rotated to make it orientation-invariant. It is computed in two steps:
  - First, the normalized values are computed as $r_i = R_i/R$.
  - Then, all values are rotated in the vector in such a way that highest values are at the center, according to a local average measure. Specifically, a given section i will be at the center if the average of all values r_j, with $j = i - 4, \ldots,$ $i + 4$, is the highest.
- Normalized radius standard deviation, s — computed over all r_i.
- Block averages, B_k — the normalized radius values are divided into six blocks; for each block k, where $k = 1, .., 6$, B_k is defined as the average of all r_i values, for $i = (k-1) \times 6 + 1, \ldots, k \times 6$.

This feature extraction strategy provides 45 features to the learning algorithm. The first 2 features (R and S) provide size information. The remaining 43 normalized features capture the shape of a segmented object, invariant to its size, translation and rotation. Figure 2 (left) shows a scene with three objects (a stapler, a pen and a ball). Figure 3 shows the normalized radius vectors for the three objects.

This method is an original proposal of the authors; one of its main advantages is that it is simple to implement. The histogram approach of Roy and Pentland (2002), of which we were initially unaware, although quite different, also seems straightforward to implement. We intend to compare the two approaches in the near future.

The communication between the student robot and human instructor is supported by the perception and action systems (for instructor input and robot feedback, respectively). At present, the communication capabilities of the robot are limited to reading the teaching options (teach, ask, correct) in a menu-based interface and displaying classification results. In the future, simple spoken language communication will be supported.

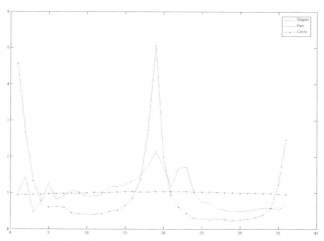

Figure 3. Normalized and rotated radius feature vectors for the three objects in Figure 2

Learning and classification capabilities are provided to the agent using a client-server approach. A new learning server, implemented as a separate process, performs both lifelong learning and classification as requested by the user. Its importance in this work is shown in the next section, which presents its design and functionality.

One-class lifelong learning

As mentioned above, one-class learning is an interesting candidate learning paradigm for such an open-ended domain as word learning. Tax (2001) describes and experimentally compares a large number of methods from the perspective of one-class learning, including Parzen density estimator, nearest neighbor, autoassociators, SVDD, LVQ, PCA, SOM, k-means and k-centers. One of the preferred methods is Support Vector Data Description (SVDD), a method that shares its foundations with the support vector classifier (Vapnik, 1995). It shows one of the best performances, provided that the training instances are not too few (e.g., less than 10). Usually, the performance on the training set is a useful indication of the performance on the test set. The performance is especially good when the training distribution is different from the target distribution. Furthermore, SVDD is particularly good at avoiding overfitting. Finally, the evaluation time is very small. We therefore selected SVDD as the base for the developed OCLL[4] system.

OCLL decomposes into two concurrent threads of processing (Figure 4). The *main thread*, supports communication with the learning client (the agent) and also runs the classification routines. The other, the *learning thread*, determines learning parameters and runs the SVDD algorithm. Having separate threads for learning and classification allows the OCLL server to execute client requests for classification and save new data for learning, while the learning thread concurrently handles learning.[5]

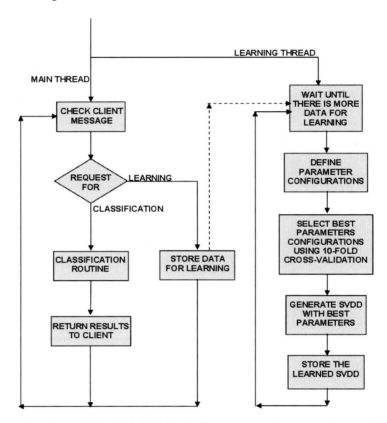

Figure 4. Flow chart of OCLL (dashed line indicates sequencing across the two different threads)

Learning

In the normal case, SVDD is trained only with positive instances of the target class. It tries to form a hypersphere around the data by finding an optimized set of support vectors. These support vectors are data points on the boundary of a hypersphere whose center is also determined through optimization. The hypersphere's center is assumed to represent the center of the data distribution itself. If outliers (negative instances) are available, they add to the performance of SVDD since, during optimization, an even tighter boundary around the data can be obtained. An introduction to SVDD's underlying mathematics is given in the Appendix.

The configuration parameters to be supplied to the SVDD algorithm are the percentage of training objects that can be considered as outliers (for better boundary description and over-fitting avoidance), *FRACREJ*, and the width parameter of the Gaussian kernel, *s* (used to map the data into a more suitable space). OCLL tries several values of *FRACREJ* and *s* and uses those with the highest performance for learning the final class description.

In the current implementation of OCLL, values of *FRACREJ* range from 1% to 11% of the training data, with an interval of 2%. This means that a total of 6 values will be tested. The maximum and minimum distance between any two training objects determines the range of values of the width parameter (for a thorough explanation on the range of values and the choice of *s* refer to Tax, 2001):

$$\min \| x_i - x_j \| \leq s \leq \max \| x_i - x_j \|$$

Since the magnitude of object features can vary significantly, the above range of values of *s* is divided into 10 parts on a logarithmic scale. This leads to 11 possible *s* values. In total, there are 66 combinations of values of *FRACREJ* and *s* for evaluation.

OCLL performs cross-validation to determine the best configuration. Specifically, for each parameter setting, 90% of the examples (randomly selected) are used for training and the remaining examples are used for performance evaluation. This is repeated 10 times, and the average performance is retained.[6] The following performance measure, which combines precision and recall values, is used:

$$\frac{2 \cdot P \cdot R}{P + R}$$

where, $P = CTP/TP$ is precision, $R = CTP/TE$ is recall, *CTP* is the number of correct target predictions, *TP* is the number of target predictions and *TE* is the number of target examples.

As mentioned previously, learning is incremental and supervised. Thus, when an object is misclassified, the instructor has the option of providing the correct class, so that class descriptions can be improved. Misclassification in this case can be of two types: either the object is inside the hyperspheres of several classes and OCLL chose the wrong class, or the object is outside the hyperspheres of all known classes. Given a correction from the user, OCLL will identify and retrain the class descriptions needing correction. Specifically, OCLL will add the misclassified object as outlier for retraining the classes whose hyperspheres contain the object.

Classification

In the standard application of SVDD class descriptions, a new object is classified as belonging to the target class if it is determined to be inside the hypersphere of the class. Using this criterion in OCLL, more than one class or none of the classes might be identified as the target, and a classification decision would be impossible to make. For this reason, a more suitable criterion has been adopted. In particular, a distance metric, called "Normalized Distance to the Center" (*NDC*) was introduced. For a given object z, $NDC(z)$ is the distance of z to the center of the hypersphere given as a fraction of its radius. It captures the relative closeness of the object from the center of each class and, therefore, enables comparison of its membership to different classes. For a particular class, the lower the value of $NDC(z)$, the closer the object is to the centre of that class. Of all the classes that have been learned, the one with the lowest $NDC(z)$ will be considered as best class candidate for object z. However, if the lowest value of $NDC(z)$ is greater than 2.0, the object is considered to be clearly outside any of the current class descriptions and thus not belonging to any class.

Experimental methodology

The word learning research surveyed above has some common features. One of them is the limitation on the number of learned words: the described approaches have been demonstrated to learn up to 12 words.

The other common feature is the fact that the number of words is pre-defined. This is contrary to the open-ended nature of the word learning domain. Then, given that the number of categories is pre-defined, the evaluation methodology usually consists of extracting certain measures on the learning process, such as semantic accuracy (Roy & Pentland, 2002), classification success (Steels & Kaplan, 2002), word-meaning grounding accuracy and object categorization accuracy (Yu, 2005). Some authors plot this type of measures versus training time. As the number of words/categories is pre-defined, the plots usually show a gradual increase of these measures and the convergence to a "final" value that the authors consider acceptable.

Robots and software agents are limited in their perceptual abilities and, therefore, cannot learn arbitrarily large numbers of categories, particularly when perception does not enable the detection of small between-category differences. The following aspects of a long-term category learning process should therefore be considered:

- Evolution: Depends on the ability of the learner to adjust category representations when a new word is introduced.
- Recovery: The discrimination performance will generally deteriorate with the introduction of a new word. The time spent in system evolution until correcting and adjusting all current categories defines recovery. Recovery is based on classification errors and corresponding corrective feedback.
- Breakpoint: Inability of the learner to recover and evolve when a new category is introduced.

A well-defined teaching protocol can facilitate the comparison of different approaches as well as the assessment of future improvements. With that in mind, along with the evolution, recovery and breakpoint aspects just described, the teaching protocol of Figure 5 is proposed.

---

introduce $Class_0$;
$n = 1$;
repeat
{
    introduce $Class_n$;
    $k = 0$;
    repeat
    {
        Evaluate and correct classifiers;
        $k \leftarrow k + 1$;
    } **until** ((average precision > precision threshold **and** $k \geq n$) **or**
               (user sees no improvement in precision)));
    $n \leftarrow n + 1$;
} **until** (user sees no improvement in precision).

Figure 5. Teaching protocol used for performance evaluation

This protocol is applicable for any open-ended class learning domain. For every new class the instructor introduces, the average precision of the whole system is calculated by performing classification on all classes for which data descriptions have already been learned. Average precision is calculated over the last $3 \times n$ classification results (n being the number of classes that have already been introduced). The precision of a single classification is either 1 (correct class) or 0 (wrong class). When the number of classification results since the last time a new class was introduced, k, is greater or equal to n, but less than $3 \times n$, the average of all results is used. The criterion that indicates that the system is ready to accept a new object class is based on the precision threshold. However, the evaluation/correction phase continues until a local maximum is reached.

Experimental results

Experiments were conducted according to the protocol proposed above. The set of words (object category names) and the set of training objects were not established in advance. As categories were learned, new objects were fetched from the surrounding office environment and used to introduce new categories. In the first experiment (already presented in Seabra Lopes & Chauhan, 2006), new categories were introduced in the following sequence:

Pen – 5 different pens were used for teaching
Stapler – 1 object of this class
Ball – 2 circular objects
Mobile – 3 objects
Key – 2 objects
Box – 2 objects
TiltedCup – 1 object
Rubber – 1 object
CoffeeCup – 1 object
StapleRemover – 1 object

In later experiments, these objects and categories were used again, in different sequences. In some experiments, it was possible to introduce two additional categories, bringing the total to 12:

ScrewDriver – 1 object
Plug – 1 object

Figure 6 shows instances of the used object classes. Natural light variation significantly affects the quality of the images collected from the camera, because the scene is just in front of a window.

Obtained results are graphically presented in Figures 7 and 8. They respectively show the evolution of *classification precision* and *learning efficiency* against the number of question/correction iterations. Efficiency is defined as the ratio between the obtained classification precision and the precision of a random classifier. In each iteration, the precision of the random classifier is computed based on the number of currently introduced classes. Points of high instability of the measures in Figures 7 and 8 in most cases indicate the introduction of a new class.

Classification for an object of the first class (*pen*) was correct in the first attempt. This means a single iteration was enough to reach a precision of 100%. Similarly, for the second class, in the minimum number of iterations (at least n iterations for n classes, as defined above) maximum precision was obtained. On

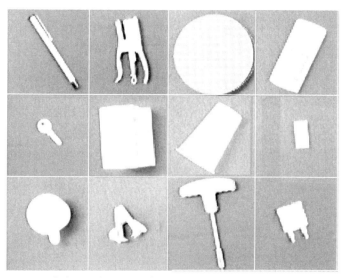

Figure 6. Instances of object classes used in experiments

the introduction of the third class *(ball)*, although starting at 100%, precision continuously dropped to 50%, before it recovered to a value above the threshold.[7] For the next classes, the pattern remained similar: precision degrades at the introduction of the new class and then recovers after a number of question/correction iterations.

On the introduction of the 10th class *(staple remover)*, precision started at 100%, then dropped to values between 20% and 50%, remaining there for many iterations. As can be seen at the end of the graphs of Figures 7 and 8, classification precision and learning efficiency seem to have stabilized. No considerable improvement in these measures could be noticed over time. Here the instructor concluded that, on the extracted set of features and for the above set of classes, the learning capacity of the student had reached its breakpoint.

It should be noted that, most of the time, learning efficiency is above 2.0, and its average is 4.3. This means that precision is significantly above the random classifier precision throughout the whole experiment. Another important observation can be made. While classification precision seems to follow a decreasing trend as the number of introduced classes increases, learning efficiency follows an increasing trend almost until the breakpoint class.

In OCLL, each correction leads to the introduction of new positive and negative examples. For each new class introduced, Figure 9 shows the total number of outliers and positive examples added to the system to achieve the precision threshold. It can be seen from this figure that introduction of the last two classes

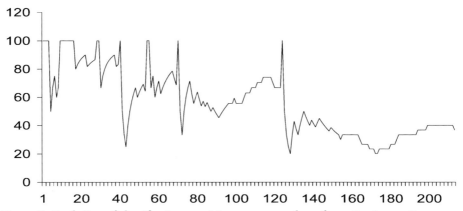

Figure 7. Evolution of classification precision versus number of question/correction iterations

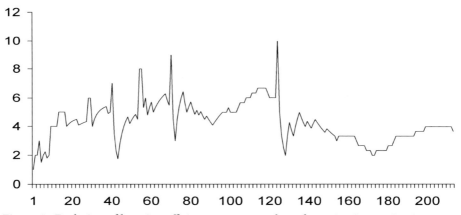

Figure 8. Evolution of learning efficiency versus number of question/correction iterations

adds high numbers of outliers as well as positive examples. In comparison to the initial eight classes, the number of misclassifications after the 9th class was introduced shows a substantial increase. In other words, it became increasingly difficult for the system to reach the precision threshold. Eventually, on the 10th class the system reached its breakpoint. A collective analysis of Figures 7–9 shows an association between the number of iterations required for reaching the precision threshold and the number of outliers and positive examples needed before the system reached the precision threshold. For the first eight classes, the system shows fast evolution of precision and efficiency. The number of examples and outliers

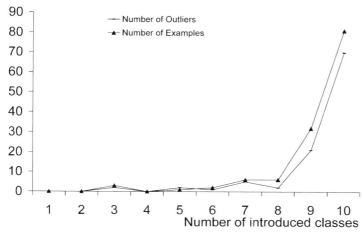

Figure 9. Number of outliers and positive examples added after each new class was introduced in the experiment of Figures 7–8

that was necessary to add after introducing those classes are also relatively few. On the other hand, for the 9th and 10th classes, it took a long time to reach the precision threshold (not achieved after introducing the 10th class) and the number of outliers and target examples introduced to the system showed a sharp increase.

Table 1 shows the number of outliers and positive examples stored for each class after the system reached the breakpoint. As can be observed, the number of outliers in some classes (*Box* and *TiltedCup*) far outweighs the number of target examples.

Table 1. Final number of target and outlier examples in each class (for the experiment of Figures 7–8)

Object class	Target	Outliers
Pen	17	18
Stapler	24	1
Ball	30	7
Mobile	27	1
Key	22	1
Box	14	49
TiltedCup	17	40
Rubber	24	1
CoffeeCup	19	1
StapleRemover	14	9

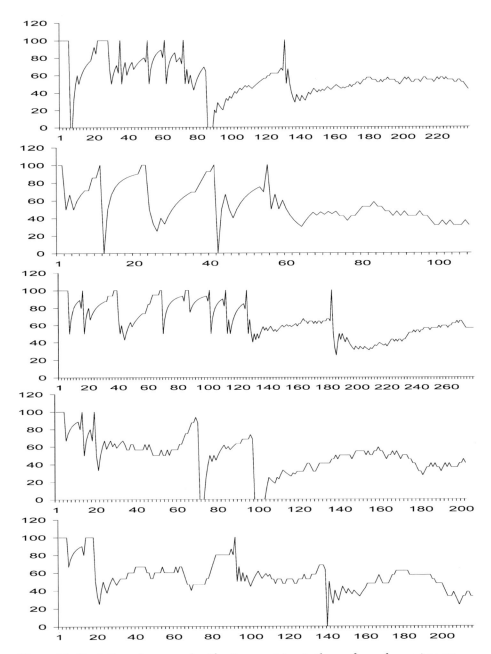

Figure 10. Evolution of average classification precision in the performed experiments. The horizontal axis is the number of question/correction iterations and vertical axis is precision. The number of introduced words is respectively: 10, 12, 6, 12, 7 and 7 (Figure 7 and then Figure 10 from top to bottom)

Tax (2001) observed that introducing a few outliers to the training data results in better class descriptions for one-class classifiers, but introducing too many deteriorates learning performance. For the first introduced classes, classification precision improved very quickly, which supports the idea that, when using few outliers, SVDD class descriptions do describe the data better than just with positive instances. However, in the long run, the number of outliers in the training data may become higher than the number of target examples. This may also limit the number of classes that the system will be able to learn.

The experiment was repeated several times (Figure 10). The object classes (and therefore the words) were the same, although some of the instances were different. The experimental set up also varied slightly, since the camera is now at a greater distance from the objects, which implies less resolution. In the first three of these experiments, the same sequence of introduction of new classes was used. Breakpoint was detected after 6 introduced classes in one case (109 iterations) and after 12 classes in the other two cases (239 and 279 iterations). Two additional experiments were carried out for different (randomly generated) sequences. In both, it was possible to reach only 7 classes (203 and 217 iterations). These experiments (Figure 10) are in line with the observations already discussed for the initial experiment.

Summary and discussion

This paper addresses word learning for human–robot interaction. Instead of following a computationalist approach strictly focused on finding invariances for category learning, a more integrational approach was adopted, which is in line with previous work in our group (Seabra Lopes, 2002; Seabra Lopes & Connell, 2001b; Seabra Lopes et al., 2005). In this approach, the robot's user is explicitly included in the language acquisition process. Through mechanisms of shared attention and corrective feedback, the human user, acting as instructor or mediator, can help the agent ground the words used to refer to objects that it finds in its environment. This is consistent with current views on distributed cognition, distributed language and external symbol grounding (Cowley, 2007a).

The present work was carried out with a particular concern for the fact that word learning is an open-ended domain. This means it cannot be realistic to address the problem as if there is a pre-defined set of words, although that is the typical approach to the problem. A vocabulary can grow as long as the perceptual and cognitive abilities of an agent allow it to grow. In characterizing vocabulary growth, aspects of evolution of category representations, recovery from confusion after the introduction of new words and breakpoint are important. Based on these considerations, a novel experimental methodology was proposed for evaluating a word learning method, from the first acquired words until the limits of the method. This methodology can be useful for comparing the word learning capabilities of different agents as well to assess research progress with respect to scaling-up to larger vocabularies.

While not strictly focused on the problem of finding invariances for category learning, this problem was addressed with a new approach based on the *one-class learning* paradigm and, in particular, on support-vector data descriptions. More importantly, the learning aspects were also addressed at a more integrational level. A learning module, OCLL, acting as "learning server" for category formation and evolution, was implemented and integrated in the agent. The way OCLL works has several important properties: It is supervised, on-line, opportunistic, incremental, concurrent and capable of meta-learning. Since all of these properties are required for the learning computations, some of them (e.g., supervised, opportunistic) are crucial to support the dynamics of external symbol grounding.

The proposed experimental methodology was used to evaluate the performance of the agent on learning the names of several real-world office objects. From the conducted experiments, it can be concluded that the agent has the ability to incrementally evolve to include each new word presented. Classification precision falls after the introduction of new words, but quickly recovers by correcting the classifiers so that the boundaries of the respective class descriptions get modified to separate out all the different classes.

As the number of words increases, the training becomes more difficult and some class descriptions have to be corrected many times before the precision threshold is achieved. Eventually, the learning capacity of the agent reaches its breakpoint. In the different runs of experiments, this happened between the 6th and the 12th word. Although the different published works on word learning are not directly comparable to each other or to the above presented work (due to their many specificities), the results reported above are comparable to results previously reported by others with respect to the number of learned words.

These results raise several issues for discussion. The main issues are concerned with the existence of a breakpoint in the word learning capacity of a robot. The existence itself seems easy to accept. Robots are limited in their perceptual (sensors, sensor fusion, active sensing) and sensorimotor abilities and, therefore, cannot learn arbitrarily large numbers of categories, particularly when perception and action do not enable them to detect small between-category differences.

The fact that the breakpoint occurs no later than the 12th word is more problematic. A robot with such a limitation will not be of any use in environments that require language-based interaction with users. Why can't these systems learn more words and categories? In particular, why can't they learn more concrete object categories and names?

A combination of the following factors may explain the limitation:

- –   sensor limitations
- –   lack of active sensing/animate vision
- –   lack of physical interaction with the target objects
- –   lack of consideration of the affordances of objects
- –   limited interaction between the learning agent and the human caregiver
- –   inappropriate perceptual abilities and representations
- –   inappropriate category learning methods.

With respect to sensing, our agent is very limited. A single camera enables perception of target objects, and it remains in a fixed position over the objects. There is no possibility either for active/animate sensing or for sensorimotor experience with the objects. This limitation is common to most existing prototypes and models. The most notable exception is reported by Roy and Pentland (2002), who use a robotic arm and a turn-table to capture multiple views of each object. None of the surveyed systems uses physical interaction with objects to categorize them.

Moreover, because of these limitations, neither our system nor the surveyed systems are able to take into account the affordances of objects, that is, the actions and uses that they afford. Interestingly, an early explanation for the shape bias, observed in children when learning concrete object names, was based on the conjecture that shape would be a strong determiner of affordances (Rosch, 1973). This is currently a subject of investigation (Gershhoff-Stowe & Smith, 2004). Gibson (1979) also stressed the importance of affordances in visual perception. An early robotic model that categorizes affordances (the produced categories are here called proto-symbols) and uses them to guide navigation was described by Mac-Dorman, Tatani, Miyazaki and Koeda (2000).

Our approach explicitly includes the human user as instructor or mediator for the word learning process. However, in the current version, the initiative for interaction between the instructor and the artificial agent is always on the instructor's side. In the foreseeable future, we intend to integrate a robotic arm into the agent and assign it goals. In this richer scenario, the agent may also wish to ask for instructor's help to the language acquisition process. This results in a mixed-initiative interaction that allows for dual control and mutual gearing, as observed in the relation between infant and caregiver (Cowley, 2007a, 2007b).

The limitations discussed so far are concerned with the "external" component of language acquisition and symbol grounding. Meanwhile, the internal mechanisms should also be significantly improved. The learning approaches that have been used until now in most systems are either connectionist or instance-based. In the work reported above, one-class learning with support-vector data descriptions was used. All these approaches take as input collections of feature vectors representing training instances. However, it has been pointed out that feature vectors are not always the best representation for learning (Aha & Wettschereck, 1997). This is particularly the case when instances can be split into components leading to a structured/relational representation. Object categorization based on shape, as we have implemented (and is the key bias in children as well), could be better handled with relational instead of vector-based representations. That is also the assumption underlying the cognitive theory of recognition-by-components (Biederman, 1987). These ideas link to some of the literature on symbol systems and symbol grounding. For instance, the theory of "perceptual symbol systems" (Barsalou, 1999) emphasizes that a perceptual symbol represents a schematic component of a perception, and not a holistic experience. Also, the "Symbolic Theft Hypothesis" (Cangelosi & Harnad, 2000) emphasizes that complex categories can be learned more efficiently from more basic categories than directly form sensor data. Based on all these considerations, we believe that adopting component-based/relational representations is a promising research path. In this approach, more complex, composed categories would represent individual physical objects instead of primitive categories, as is usually the case.

As can be seen from this discussion, there is plenty of work for the robotics, AI and cognitive science communities concerning the development of artificial agents able to acquire extended vocabularies. Our own work will focus on improving the internal mechanisms, as well as extending the sensorimotor and interaction capabilities of the robot.

Notes

The Portuguese Research Foundation (FCT) supported this work under contract POSI/SRI/48794/2002 (project "LANGG: Language Grounding for Human–Robot Communication"), which is partially funded by FEDER. The authors would like to thank Stephen Cowley, Karl MacDorman and Armando Pinho for enlightening discussions and anonymous reviewers for many constructive and helpful comments.

1. An IEEE1394 compliant *Unibrain Fire-i digital camera* is being used.

2. The implementation of the *canny algorithm*, from the publicly available openCV library of vision routines, is used for edge detection. Other openCV functions have been used in the implementation. See http://www.intel.com/technology/computing/opencv/index.htm.

3. This is performed using a region growing algorithm.

4. The name derives from "one-class lifelong learning."

5. The OCLL server is a C++ program which runs as a single Linux process divided into two threads. An implementation of SVDD for MATLAB is in the dd-tools toolbox (Tax, 2005) publicly available at http://www-ict.ewi.tudelft.nl/~davidt/dd_tools.html. Therefore, in practice, the

SVDD algorithm runs in a separate MATLAB-based process on request of the learning thread of OCLL. The main thread saves any new training data in a file and informs the learning thread to process it. When there is no new data to process, the learning thread is waiting on a semaphore. When new data is received, the learning thread calls SVDD on the MATLAB process and waits until SVDD returns. The MATLAB process stores the learned class description in a file.

6. For this reason, the instructor must provide at least 10 examples for learning to start.

7. In these experiments, the precision threshold was set to 0.667. This ensures that, in a stable situation, there will be at least twice as many correct answers as incorrect answers, which intuitively appears to be a suitable baseline for acceptable performance.

References

Aha, D. W. & Wettschereck, D. (1997). Case-based learning: Beyond classification of feature vectors. In M. van Someren & G. Widmer (Eds.), *Proceedings of the Nineth European Conference on Machine Learning (ECML 1997)* (pp. 329–336), LNCS 1224, London, UK: Springer-Verlag.

Ameel, E., Malt, B., & Storms, G. (2006). Object naming and later lexical development. In R. Sun & N. Miyake (Eds.), *Proceedings of the 28th Annual Conference of the Cognitive Science Society* (pp. 18–23). Mahwah, NJ: Lawrence Erlbaum.

Anderson, M. L. & Perlis, D. R. (2002). Symbol systems. In Nadel, L., Chalmers, D., Culicover, P., French, B. & Goldstone, R., *Encyclopedia of Cognitive Science*, London, UK: Macmillan.

Barsalou, L. (1999). Perceptual symbol systems, *Behavioral and Brain Sciences, 22*(4), 577–609.

Bates, E., Thal, D., Finlay, B. & Clancy, B. (2002). Early language development and its neural correlates. In S. J. Segalowitz & I. Rapin (Eds.), *Handbook of neuropsychology: Child neuropsychology* (Vol. 7, pp. 69–110). Amsterdam: Elsevier.

Biederman, I. (1987). Recognition-by-components: A theory of human image understanding. *Psychological Review, 94*, 115–147.

Breazeal, C. & Scassellati, B. (2000). Infant-like social interactions between a robot and a human caregiver. *Adaptive Behavior, 8*(1), 49–74.

Brooks, R. A. (1991). Intelligence without representation. *Artificial Intelligence Journal, 47*, 139–159.

Cangelosi, A. (2005). Approaches to grounding symbols in perceptual and sensorimotor categories. In H. Cohen & C. Lefebvre (Eds.), *Handbook of Categorization in Cognitive Science* (pp. 719–737). Oxford: Elsevier Science.

Cangelosi, A. & Harnad, S. (2000). The adaptive advantage of symbolic theft over sensorimotor toil: Grounding language in perceptual categories. *Evolution of Communication, 4*(1), 117–142.

Clark, A. (1997). *Being there: Putting brain, body and world together again*. Cambridge, MA: MIT Press.

Chatila, R. (2004). The cognitive robot companion and the European 'Beyond robotics initiative'. In *Proceedings of the Sixth EAJ International Symposium on Living with Robots*. Tokyo, Japan.

Cowley, S. J. (2007a). Distributed language: Biomechanics, functions and the origins of talk. In C. Lyon, C. Nehaniv & A. Cangelosi (Eds.), *Emergence of communication and language*. Heidelberg (pp. 105–127), London: Springer.

Cowley, S. J. (2007b). How human infants deal with symbol grounding. *Interaction Studies*, 8(1), ppp-ppp.

Crystal, D. (1987). How many words? *English Today*, 12, 11–14.

Fong, T., Nourbakhsh, I. & Dautenhahn, K. (2003). A survey of socially interactive robots: Concepts, design, and applications, *Robotics and Autonomous Systems*, 42, 143–166.

Gershhoff-Stowe, L. & Smith, L. B. (2004). Shape and the first hundred nouns. *Child Development*, 74(4), 1098–1114.

Gibson, J. J. (1979). *The ecological approach to visual perception*. Boston, MA: Houghton Mifflin.

Gillette, J. Gleitman, H., Gleitman, L. & Lederer, A. (1999). Human simulations of vocabulary learning. *Cognition*, 73, 135–176.

Greco, A., Riga, T. & Cangelosi, A. (2003). The acquisition of new categories through grounded symbols: An extended connectionist model. O. Kaynak, E. Alpaydin, E. Oja and L. Xu (Eds.), *Artificial Neural Networks and Neural Information Processing — ICANN/ICONIP 2003*, Springer, pp. 773–770.

Harnad, S. (1990). The symbol grounding problem, *Physica D*, 42, 335–346.

Harnad, S., Hanson, S. J. & Lubin, J. (1991). Categorical perception and the evolution of supervised learning in neural nets. In D. W. Powers & L. Reeker (Eds.), *Working Papers of the AAAI Spring Symposium on Machine Learning of Natural Language and Ontology*, pp. 65–74.

Harnad, S., Hanson, S. J. & Lubin, J. (1995). Learned categorical perception in neural nets: Implications for symbol grounding. In V. Honavar & L. Uhr (Eds), *Symbol processors and connectionist models in artificial intelligence and cognitive modelling: Steps toward principled integration* (pp. 191–206). San Diego, CA: Academic Press.

Japkowicz, N. (1999). Are we better off without counter-examples? In *Proceedings of the First International ICSC Congress on Computational Intelligence Methods and Applications (CIMA-99)*, pp. 242–248.

Levinson, S. E., Squire, K., Lin, R. S. & McClain, M. (2005). Automatic language acquisition by an autonomous robot. *Proceedings of the AAAI Spring Symposium on Developmental Robotics*. March 21–23.

Love, N. (2004). Cognition and the language myth. *Language Sciences*, 26, 525–544.

MacDorman, K. F., Tatani, K., Miyazaki, Y. & Koeda, M. (2000). Proto-symbol emergence, *Proceedings of the 2000 IEEE/RSJ International Conference on Intelligent Robots and Systems (IROS 2000)*, Takamatsu, Japan, pp. 1619–1625.

Plunkett, K. & Sinha C. G. (1992). Connectionism and developmental theory. *British Journal of Developmental Psychology*, 10, 209–254.

Plunkett, K., Sinha, C., Moller, M. F. & Strandsby, O. (1992). Symbol grounding or the emergence of symbols? Vocabulary growth in children and a connectionist net. *Connection Science*, 4(3–4), 293–312.

Polikar, R., Udpa, L., Udpa, S. S. & Honavar, V. (2001). Learn++: An incremental learning algorithm for supervised neural networks. *IEEE Transactions on Systems, Man, and Cybernetics, Part C*, 31(4), 497–508.

Roy, D. & Pentland, A. (2002). Learning words from sights and sounds: A computational model. *Cognitive Science*, 26, 113–146.

Rosch, E. (1973). On the internal structure of perceptual and semantic categories. In T. E. Moore (Ed.), *Cognitive development and the acquisition of language* (pp. 111–144). San Diego, CA: Academic Press.

Russell, S. & Norvig, P. (2003). *Artificial intelligence: A modern approach* (Rev. ed.). Upper Saddle River, NJ: Prentice-Hall.

Sales, N. J. & Evans, R. G. (1995). An approach to solving the symbol grounding problem: Neural networks for object naming and retrieval. *Proceedings of the International Conference on Cooperative Multimodal Communications (CMC-95)*. Eindhoven, The Netherlands.

Samuelson, L. & Smith, L. B. (2005). They call it like they see it: Spontaneous naming and attention to shape. *Developmental Science, 8*(2), 182–198.

Seabra Lopes, L. (2002). Carl: From situated activity to language-level interaction and learning. In *Proceedings of 2002 IEEE/RSJ International Conference on Intelligent Robots and Systems (IROS 2000)* (pp. 890–896). Lausanne, Switzerland.

Seabra Lopes, L. & Chauhan, A. (2006). One-class lifelong learning approach to grounding. *Workshop on External Symbol Grounding. Book of Abstracts and Papers* (pp. 15–23). University of Plymouth, Plymouth, UK.

Seabra Lopes, L. & Connell, J. H. (Eds.) (2001a). *Semisentient Robots* special issue of *IEEE Intelligent Systems, 16*(5).

Seabra Lopes, L. & Connell, J. H. (2001b). Semisentient robots: Routes to integrated intelligence. *IEEE Intelligent Systems* (special issue on *Semisentient Robots*, L. Seabra Lopes & J.H. Connell, Eds.), *16*(5), 10–14.

Seabra Lopes, L. & Wang, Q. H. (2002). Towards grounded human–robot communication. In *Proceedings of 11th IEEE International Workshop on Robot and Human Interactive Communication* (Ro-Man 2002), pp. 312–318.

Seabra Lopes, L., Teixeira, A. J. S., Quinderé, M. & Rodrigues, M. (2005). From robust spoken language understanding to knowledge acquisition and management. *Proceeding of Interspeech 2005* (pp. 3469–3472). Lisbon, Portugal.

Smith, L. B. & Samuelson, L. (2006). An attentional learning account of the shape bias. *Developmental Psychology 42*(6), 1339–1343.

Steels, L. (2001). Language games for autonomous robots. *IEEE Intelligent Systems* (special issue on *Semisentient Robots*, L. Seabra Lopes and J. H. Connell, Eds.), *16*(5), 16–22.

Steels, L. & Kaplan, F. (2002). AIBO's first words: The social learning of language and meaning, *Evolution of Communication, 4*(1), 3–32.

Talmy, L. (2000). *Toward a cognitive semantics: Concept structuring systems (language, speech and communication)*. Cambridge, MA: The MIT Press.

Tax, D. M. J. (2001). *One-class classification: Concept learning in the absence of counter-examples*. Unpublished doctoral dissertation, Technische Universiteit Delft, The Netherlands.

Tax, D. M. J (2005). *DD Tools — The Data Description Toolbox for MATLAB. Version 1.4.1*, Technische Universiteit Delft, The Netherlands.

Thrun, S. (1996). *Explanation-based neural network learning: A lifelong learning approach*. Boston, MA: Kluwer.

Turing, A. (1950). Computing machinery and intelligence. *Mind, 59*, 433–460.

Vapnik, V. (1995). *The nature of statistical learning theory*. New York: Springer-Verlag.

Wang, Q. & Seabra Lopes, L. (2004). Visual object recognition through one-class learning. *Proceedings of International Conference on Image Analysis and Recognition (ICIAR 2004)*, Part I, LNCS 3211, Springer, pp. 463–469.

Yoshida, H. & Smith, L. B. (2005). Linguist cues enhance the learning of perceptual cues. *Psychological Science, 16* (2), 90–95.

Yu, C. (2005). The emergence of links between lexical acquisition and object categorization: A computational study. *Connection Science, 17*(3–4), 381–397.

Appendix — Mathematical background

SVDD forms a hypersphere around the data by finding an optimized set of support vectors. These support vectors are data points on the boundary of a hypersphere whose center is also determined through optimization. The optimization process, that determines the center and support vectors, attempts to minimize two errors:

– Empirical error — percentage of misclassified training samples.
– Structural error — defined as R^2, where R is the radius of the hypersphere, must be minimized with respect to center a and constraints $\|x_i - a\|^2 \le R^2$, for every training object x_i.

In the ideal case (no noise), all training objects can be included in the hypersphere and therefore the empirical error will be 0. In practical applications, however, this may result in over-fitting. Better results can be obtained with not much extra computational expense if a kernel is introduced to get a better data description (Tax, 2001). In addition, if a set of outliers (negative instances) is known, it adds to the performance of SVDD since, during optimization, an even tighter boundary around the data can be obtained. From (Tax, 2001), the final error L to be optimized is given as:

$$L = \sum_i \alpha_i K(x_i, x_i) - \sum_{i,j} \alpha_i \alpha_j K(x_i, x_j)$$

with the following constraints on Lagrange multipliers:

$$\forall i, 0 \le \alpha_i \le C$$

$$\sum_i \alpha_i = 1 \text{ and } a = \sum_i \alpha_i x_i$$

C gives the tradeoff between the volume of the description and the errors. The kernel K maps the data into a more suitable space. Although the choice of kernel is data dependent, in most applications a Gaussian kernel will produce good results. Tax (2001) gives a thorough explanation of the performance benefits of this kernel. It is defined as:

$$K(x_i, x_j) = \exp\left(\frac{-|x_i - x_j|^2}{s^2}\right)$$

where s is the width parameter of the kernel.

Class descriptions provide the support vectors and their respective α_i and s. In the standard application of SVDD class descriptions, the criterion for classifying any new object z as target is:

$$\sum_i \alpha_i K(z, x_i) > \frac{1}{2}(B - R)^2$$

where, $B = 1 + \sum_{i,j} \alpha_i \alpha_j K(x_i, x_j)$ and R is the radius.

In OCLL, given the need to decide which class is more suitable for a particular instance, it was necessary to define the following normalized distance metric:

$$NDC(z) = \frac{\sqrt{B - 2\sum_i \alpha_i K(z, x_i)}}{R}$$

NDC (Normalized Distance to the Center) is the distance of an object z to the center of the hypersphere given as a fraction of its radius R.

How human infants deal with symbol grounding

Stephen J. Cowley
School of Psychology, University of Hertfordshire and University of
KwaZulu-Natal, South Africa

Taking a distributed view of language, this paper naturalizes symbol grounding.
Learning to talk is traced to — not categorizing speech sounds — but events
that shape the rise of human-style autonomy. On the *extended symbol hypothesis*,
this happens as babies integrate micro-activity with slow and deliberate adult
action. As they discover social norms, *intrinsic motive formation* enables them
to reshape co-action. Because infants link affect to contingencies, dyads develop
norm-referenced routines. Over time, infant doings become *analysis amenable*.
The caregiver of a nine-month-old may, for example, prompt the baby to fetch
objects. Once she concludes that the baby uses 'words' to understand what she
says, the infant can use this belief in orienting to more abstract contingencies.
New cognitive powers will develop as the baby learns to act in ways that are
consistent with a caregiver's false belief that her baby uses 'words.'

Keywords: agency, distributed cognition, distributed language, early child
development, epigenetic robotics, intersubjectivity, language acquisition,
symbol grounding

Introduction

Church, Turing and Chomsky emphasised resemblances between human utterances and formal symbol strings. By focusing on syntax, they found striking
parallels between language users and physical symbol systems. In the long run,
however, recognition of semantic differences led to the demise of purely symbolic models. First, since form-based simulations throw no light on understanding (Searle, 1980), they are of limited use in modelling mind. Second, in spite of
Turing's (1950) exhortations, it is difficult to design machines that *learn* linguistic
forms. As a consequence, the external grounding of understanding has come to be

recognised. To solve the symbol grounding problem (SGP), representations must connect with both classes of referent and the appropriate word-forms (Harnad, 1990). While some action needs no symbols (e.g., Brooks, 1999), agents that interact with an environment can develop symbol-systems that give flexibility to their perception and action. Much can be gained from using action-guided representations (Anderson, 2003a, 2003b).

In their review of attempts to solve the SGP, Taddeo and Floridi (2005) conclude that representational, semi-representational and nonrepresentational models can all make symbols *seem* value-laden. However, this impression relies on human interpretation, because the manipulation of the symbols is hard-coded. This "semantic commitment," they conclude, means that the SGP remains unsolved. Even less progress has been made in mapping symbols to verbal patterns. To ground formal properties of a burst of speech (e.g., *pferd*), agents need to categorise human expression.[1] It is, however, difficult to derive word-forms from natural speech. Further, when approached from a practical perspective (Seabra Lopes & Chaudhun, 2007) words and perception are dealt with together. Simpler solutions, it seems, use human teaching rather than categorisation. Further, it has been found that formal patterns can warp the perception of even artificial agents (e.g., Cangelosi et al., 2002; Steels & Belpaeme, 2005). Today, therefore, there is growing interest in semiotic approaches which, it is hoped, can overcome the limits of formal modelling.

Naturalising symbol grounding

Instead of focusing on the logic of symbol grounding, I aim to naturalise the problem. By taking a developmental view, I show how infants ground action-guided representations into language in its broadest sense. While working conceptually, my objective is to encourage engineers to build language-using robots. In reinterpreting empirical work, I trace human symbol grounding to the agent's history of co-ordinating with others. Thus, newborns have become quite different kinds of agents by the time have developed into infants who are able to ground representations into objects. This agency is further transformed by the time that they come to hear utterances as 'words'. As agency changes, moreover, so do the functions of expression. While small babies rely on affect-based dynamics, coordinating prompts them to use human signals in ways that impose norm-based structure on the world.[2] Thus, around their first birthday, infants may begin to use sound-patterns that are heard as, for example, *milk* or *gone*. Using their grasp of situations, they rely on adults to interpret their utterances. Learning to talk thus occurs as infants and caregivers become skilled at acting under dual control (Cowley et al., 2004;

Cowley, 2006a). Over time, dependence on innate biases gives way to increased use of body-world co-ordination and, later, to reliance on a nascent self.

Naturalising the process of symbol grounding emphasises how brains and bodies are co-ordinated during joint behaviour. While the importance of social-coordination is often recognised, it is often forgotten that the body enacts language (and other expression). Indeed, infant behaviour is compatible both with Cangelosi's (2006) emphasis on social factors and with Steels and Belpaeme's (2005) emphasis on how a robot can learn to integrate co-ordination with perception (cf. MacDorman, 1999). Further, if social co-ordination anchors robot categories, similar processes may well alter human agency. Below, I suggest that the affective properties of utterances prompt infants to apply new kinds of leverage to caregivers. In emphasising how activity is co-ordinated (see Spurrett & Cowley, 2004), I stress that babies use *culturally* evolved patterns. While initially relying on affect, they come to grasp how values and beliefs play out in a range of situations (e.g., "Be quiet!"). Interaction gives way to co-action that provides a basis for speech-mediated communication and, later, context-free conversation. Pursuing this, I reinterpret old findings against a new perspective. By appealing to the concept of *distributed language*, I show how human agency arises from events under the dual control of mother and caregiver. This allows the division of symbol grounding into phases. While infants initially align behaviour to the sound-patterns of a community, they later develop ways of acting that sustain belief in *language* (and *words*). After summarising this as the extended symbol hypothesis, I sketch later changes and explain how the model applies to machines.

Distributed Language

Following Saussure (1916), linguists often conceptualise language in terms of 'use.' Instead of regarding talk as behaviour, they posit code-like forms (or signs) as constituting 'language.' While this view arose in contesting 19th century work, its logic permeates most 20th century theory (Matthews, 2001). The code view characterises Saussure's (1916) view of language-systems (*langues*) and dominates appeals to habits (Bloomfield, 1933), utterances (Harris, 1951), functions (Halliday & Matthieson, 1999; Martinet, 1960) and form-based systems (Chomsky, 1965; Jackendoff, 2002; Lakoff & Johnston, 1980; Pinker, 1994). In each theory, language is identified with formal units. As in folk psychology, language is reduced to verbal patterns whose forms are independent of history, affect and motor activity (viz. acts of utterance).[3] Code models thus distinguish the patterns that are represented (forms) from the representing agent. In so doing, they posit that cognition is separable from embodied action and perception. This epistemic conception of mind (Cowley & Spurrett, 2003) enables language to be modelled in terms of input/output processes. However, the price paid for this, is high: it implies that how babies act, feel and move has no relevance for learning that exploits (what we call) linguistic forms.

On the distributed view, language is embodied, individual and cultural (Cowley, 2006a). Agents can reflect on the significations of words or, in 19th century terms, draw on historical facts. With time, we learn to reflect on words and, by so doing, to stabilise their value. We thus resemble linguists who, as Paul (1891) observes, rely on how words are "historically derived" (p. xlviii). Language thus permits reflection, unites individual and cultural experience and, as a result, has a constitutive role in behaviour. In recent terms, language links a meshwork of heterogeneous elements (e.g., utterances, texts, pop songs) that emerge as a result of creative drift. As DeLanda (1997, p. 39) says of towns, language is an "interlocking system of complementary… functions" that are spread across space and time. In language, bodies connect a meshwork whose basis is simultaneously social, historical and individual. Like a city, language grows as well-established structures like hierarchies and paradigms come to be articulated in new ways. Most notably, in the last few thousand years, artefacts that include writing instruments, documents, books, and computers have transformed oral practices (Donald, 1991; Clark, 1997). These too interlock cultural patterns while remaining subject to the constraints of human evolution and development.

In a distributed meshwork, no appeal is made to external languages.[4] When learning to talk, infants have to discover ways of integrating their own feeling and moving with that of others. They develop skilled behaviour that extends already grounded symbols. Much depends on how these action-guided representations affect the infant's developing brain. Intrinsic motive formation (Trevarthen, 1998; Trevarthen & Aitken, 2001) exploits how caregivers spread information in getting babies to attend to aspects of the environment. Far from facing a problem of symbol grounding, action-grounded symbols function as cognitive resources. Higher order structures develop out of joint activity that connects an infant's lower-order representations with how adults enact what they are trying to do. In line with Davidson (1986) and the later Wittgenstein (1953), language is an intrinsic part of our cultural life. At the neural level, perception and action connect mammalian representations (symbols) with systems that motivate acting (and thinking). Over time, infants come to hear sounds that can be analysed formally even if, early on, they rely heavily on their affective value. Language is hybrid or, in Love's (2007) terms, both analogue and digital (i.e., categorical). Indeed, this dual nature is crucial in learning both to talk and to acquire many other skills.

In reporting conversational events, for example, we can describe how *words* and *tone* contribute to their particular sense. Both features matter because our wordings depend on both the words actually spoken and displays of affect. Language uses cognitive dynamics that alter how others feel, think and act. While verbal patterns constrain language and sense-making, their roots lie in micro-temporal dynamics.[5]

There are many reasons for adopting a distributed view. First, talk is both dynamical and dependent on rate-independent switches. While the ability to repeat what we hear depends on patterns, dynamics are needed to render incomplete information into a new structure. Second, this is compatible with the physics of symbols (Pattee, 2001). Far from needing to implement rules, infants can become rule-followers by drawing on real-time dynamics. Their future action may depend on, not represented wordings, but a history of co-ordination. To engage with language, infants' bodies and brains may attune to contingencies that are normatively constrained. Third, natural history can draw on a co-evolutionary process. Rather than posit a syntactic 'core' to language, weight falls on sensorimotor toil (Cangelosi et al., 2002). Learning to talk is thus grounded in how affect shapes the dyad's use of biomechanics. Fourth, linguistic 'forms' become entities guaranteed, not by brains, but talk about talk (and how this *linguistic reflexivity* is institutionalised in dictionaries, grammars, spell-check programs, etc.). For the modeller, this has advantages. Artificial agents can use programs, spreading activation and extended symbol systems that use a history of co-ordination. New importance falls on building machines that, like infants, align to human expectations. Although the behavioural capacities for meaning-making "*appear* to be symbolic" (Harnad, 1990, p. 337; my italics), their basis may lie in co-ordinated dynamics. Fifth and finally, the distributed perspective fits conversational facts. For example, Cowley (1997) describes an utterance "*marrone*" that is heard as "how can that possibly be chalk?" While based on neither the syntax nor semantics of *marrone* (Italian for 'brown'), an exquisitely timed vocal duet enacts understanding. Just as in using an abacus, bodies exploit both dynamics and relations between virtual resources (words or numbers). To discover verbal patterns, an infant does not rely on hearing words, but on how adults grasp what the infant and adult are doing together.

Co-action and the emergence of the person

A physical symbol system changes its powers, first, by altering how it operates on symbols that stand in for aspects of the world. Second, it uses these operations (including perception and action) to re-categorise the perceived environment. This same logic applies in grounding symbols into, say, a simulated mushroom world or displays of colour. Applied to verbal patterns, however, a different logic applies. This is because, the multidimensional and fluctuating complexity of the speech stream relates indirectly to word-forms. Symbols are not simply grounded in the real-world objects, events, and relations they are supposed to represent but also in the continuous vocal fluctuations that contribute to co-action. Indeed, it is gratuitous to assume that babies use speech to develop explicit representations of linguistic forms. While signals (e.g., Morse code) *could* be used to develop something like a notation, speech lacks the necessary salient units.[6] Empirically, it consists neither of words nor phonological units but is, rather, a fluctuating set of multidimensional patterns (Port & Leary, 2005). Segmental structure is an analytical product and, for a baby, less salient than prosodic and voice quality patterns. Why should an infant seek out speech sounds? It is thus more parsimonious to seek the bases of learning to talk in expressive dynamics. Because language spreads across bodies, infants can use caregiver affect together with how, in real time, adults construe the ways in which infants express themselves.

Multimodal expression not only makes certain patterns salient but also imbues them with expressive value. Caregiver expression, moreover, prompts babies to change behaviour and develop their own motivational systems. Given the distributed nature of language, they can derive their powers from co-ordinating with caregivers who integrate verbal, vocal, visible and tactile expression with what is happening. Full-bodied resources serve, initially, in learning to inhibit crying and, later, to track and use features such as caregiver smiles and frowns. Affect thus enables babies to identify the likely results of their response to the caregiver's expression. While this social learning occurs under dual control, it is otherwise compatible with Piaget's view of sensorimotor development. Neural structures can be said to arise from processes of *accommodation* that develop as an infant copes with the environment. Agency changes as the infant exploits physical patterns. When learning under dual control, caregiver reactions to infant appearance and behaviour prompt the baby to use what Piaget would call *assimilation* in developing a "sense of persons" (Legerstee, 2005). Events depend on cycles of orientation and re-orientation where behavioural invariances are less salient than affect and timing. Moments feature vocalisations that are accompanied by smiles and frowns among other things. These come to be associated with contingencies that will both influence current activity and, in the long term, alter infant motive formation.[7] Strange as it may sound, infants exploit what they learn about social situations and, specifically, the "setting." They come to exploit what caregivers believe, for example, as they accede to demands for silence. In human symbol grounding, therefore, much depends on the caregiver's way of presenting situations. This, in turn, affects motive formation, ensuring that social development occurs slowly. For the purposes of this paper, social development is most usefully viewed as falling into two stages:

- infants align behaviour to sound patterns favoured locally
- they develop ways of acting that sustain belief in *language* (or *words*)

By the time children enter school, they treat words as indexing (relatively) stable meanings. Below, however, I focus on the earliest phases.

Learning to talk depends on a distributed linguistic meshwork in which sensorimotor activity becomes sensitised to both affect and shared use of social norms. The infant develops skills by orienting to caregiver behaviour and, later, discovers that others believe in *words*.[8] Early on, brains need only sustain action that can be *described* by the code metaphor. To say, *more* (or *bikkik gon*), the child neither needs phonological nor semantic representations but a capacity to use situated experience in deciding how to vocalise. The baby integrates what can be perceived with expressive action. Later, as a fully fledged person, it will take the circular view that, as a member of Community X, it uses the words of Language X. First, however, the infant must learn to use situations to get what it wants. Since this depend on how adults interpret utterance acts, the child uses the *adult's* language stance in mimicking vocal patterns. To adult ears, of course, it acquires Language X. In fact, however, the baby uses vocalisation to connect contingencies with caregiver expression and how *de facto* interpretation bears on social norms. The process falls into the following stages:

- Living at a body-world boundary (0–6 weeks)
- Early self-implicating behaviour (6–12 weeks)
- Early self-directed behaviour (4–9 months)
- Early self-regulating behaviour (9–12 months)

Using inner motives (action-guided symbols) together with how caregivers strive to control events, the baby constructs its agency. Dyads live a history of interaction where routines emerge from shifting dual control. Perceptions of how adults enact beliefs trigger infant movements based on the dyad's previous experience. By four months, infants begin to use culture in response to caregivers wants (e.g., *hold your tongue*). Capacities for body-world interaction thus develop alongside social skills as infants discover how expression can be used. The growing use of social norms *extends* action-guided symbols.[9] Gradually, co-action enables the baby to motivate the caregiver to re-structuring what they do. The dyad develop games or formats while, in solitary settings, the child learns about the physical world. Towards the end of the first year, the child connects its sense of persons with object knowledge.

By linking norm-based patterns with actions on objects, it comes up with new ways of engaging with the caregiver. It develops as a self-regulator who can become skilled in getting others to do things.

Getting started

Caregivers attempt to stimulate co-action even with newborns. They seek to get babies to respond like 'little persons.' This probably goes some way to explaining Meltzoff and Moore's (1981) finding that newborns respond in kind to a few human expressions. For example, minutes after birth, they can react mimetically to tongue protrusions (Kugiumutzakis, 1999). The function of these imitative capacities depends on the somatic marking of adult response. Affective comeback leads to increased co-ordination where adults seek to re-evoke previous infant response. At times, of course, this will prime the baby for future events. As with early tongue protrusion, this is likely to depend, in part, on parental and cultural views. Given its sensitivity to affect, the infant draws on contingencies. What a baby does in the future depends on *de facto* judgments about events at the body-world boundary.

Babies are active systems. Newborns actively *prefer* speech that has voice quality features correlated with their mothers and the rhythmical patterns of her cultural group (Karmiloff & Karmiloff-Smith, 2001; Legerstee, 2005). They elicit affective expressions that bear a cultural stamp. Although it is not clear when parental beliefs begin to shape behaviour, adult come-back soon begins to encourage, reward and disappoint. By the age of three months, babies and adults exploit what Trevarthen (1979) calls *primary intersubjectivity.* They become self-implicating by, for example, developing *personal* characteristics and, even if blind, co-ordinating movements to adult vocal rhythms (Tønsberg & Hauge, 1996). For example, as discussed below, they may draw on cultural signals to fall silent at an adult's behest. This is, perhaps, the breakthrough: the baby's control systems pick up culturally-specific cues concerning what is wanted. Infant biomechanics gradually sensitise to how caregivers enact local norms. Drawing on operant conditioning, their brains develop higher-level motives that control lower-level mimetic activity (Trevarthen, 1998; Trevarthen & Aitken, 2001). Infants develop a style of autonomy that depends on value-guided co-action.

Talking to babies: From co-action to alignment

Co-action is the basis for all social development. Unlike in much interaction with the nonhuman world, rewards are associated not only with physical events but also how these relate to culturally-valued contingencies. Thus the neural systems that drive infant action (and inhibition) become sensitised to cultural norms or apparently arbitrary forms of signalling. While depending, in part, on hard-wired systems such as those used in smiling and gaze, the result is situation-sensitive action. Once co-action becomes established, events connect micro-timing, experience and, at times, caregiver interpretation. This ensures that the self-implicating infant begins to act in ways typical of persons. For example, a routine that emerges under dual control allows a three-month-old baby to stop crying (Cowley et al., 2004). What happens arises as behaviour is co-ordinated across (at least) two time domains. While the baby's inhibitory response picks up on micro-features of interaction, the caregiver structures events in the slow domain of deliberate action. Further, this dual temporal structure gives co-action a flexibility that can prompt a baby to sensitise to caregiver attributions. For example, in one family, adults may reward infants who cry, say, in supermarkets. Many babies use contingencies to act in ways that are rewarded in such settings.

Cultural norms (e.g., belief in fun and/or respect) both meet adult expectations (when it suits the baby) and help the baby to develop a personality. When Trevarthen (1979; 1998) and Bråten (1988) first noted the intrinsic motives of babies, they appealed to neural systems that sensitise to the doings of a caregiver-in-the-niche. In contrast, Stern (1977) and Kaye (1982) sought to explain the events in terms of attunement. Regardless of theory, however, the infant's motives form in response to its evaluation of social, cognitive and emotional aspects of co-action. Dyads act according to preferences and motives that reflect what caregivers attribute to infants. Thus, constraints, such as the caregiver's beliefs, that are opaque to the baby can shape the course of co-action. By integrating events across timescales, social learning sets off spiralling changes in infant reactions to, for example, voice quality and prosody. If we consider twins, they begin to show distinctive personalities when, as infants, they become self-implicating. This is also when cultural differences emerge (Cowley et al., 2004; Trevarthen, 1988). Caregivers interpret previous experience of co-action through a cultural lens, and it affects their treatment of babies. There is variability both within and across cultures with regard to how caregivers respond to a baby judged to be sick, naughty or tired. Babies thus learn from more than the words that can be heard. Further, while children understand little, parents nurture intelligent response with speech that is also affective expression (*child-directed speech*). The baby's inner symbols are further extended as the functional value of caregiver activity comes to be related to judgements of infant *understanding*. Indeed, what is most extraordinary about human babies, which are hyper-social by the standards of the animal realm, is that they come to exploit signs of culture even before they act in self-directing ways.

In the fourth month, infants typically begin to reach for objects. It is striking that this self-directing behaviour develops in infants who have well-established situation and culture-relevant skills. Self-directed activity develops in a self-implicating infant who has already attuned to cultural settings. Thus while Western caregiver-infants dyads may focus on fun, in Africa weight is also given to activity around, for example, movements resembling song and dance (Cowley, 2003). This is especially marked in the formats that, by the middle of the year, dominate a baby's social life (Bruner, 1978). Strikingly, however, this is also a period in which attention to objects largely eclipses interest in social activity. Where possible, this attention to objects helps babies learn about their tangible and oral properties. While also gaining mastery of vocalisations (Oller, 2000), this may be independent of social motives. Rather it seems related to sensorimotor skills (e.g., sitting and crawling) and preferences for, say, what to suck. It should not be thought, however, that self-directing infants are asocial. Alongside body-world interaction they continue to build formats for co-action. Caregivers, moreover, link norms with biomechanics in, for example, seeking to prevent *bad habits* (e.g., *eating sand*). Self-directing babies are primarily focused on grounding symbols into the perceived world. At the same time, how caregivers use expression to control what happens influences the ways in which settings are seen.

At the end of the first year, children find new ways of exerting leverage on caregivers. Once again, they exploit manifest attitudes but, in this phase, connect these with the perceived properties of objects. Thus, in *social-referencing* (Campos & Sternberg, 1981; Striano & Rochat, 2000), the caregiver's dynamics may be used, for example, in deciding whether to venture beyond a visual cliff. This self-regulating behaviour, it seems, links object-perception with a history of social experience. Adult responses make the behaviour, in Cowley and Spurrett's (2003) terms, *analysis amenable*. It becomes possible to adduce new mentalistic reasons in accounting for what the baby does (e.g., "He thought that it was dangerous"). In this 'nine-month revolution' (Tomasello, 1999), a baby becomes self-regulating. What Trevarthen and Hubley (1978) call *secondary intersubjectivity* develops or, in our terms, object perception connects with a sense of persons.

By their first birthday, children regulate activity by using (what adults call) words and gestures. Adult analysis leads to behaviour change that, once again, spurs learning. Further, since thinking involves the slow domain of wordings, children find that inhibiting micro-activity opens up new opportunities. For example, Cowley (2007) describes how Luke, a nine-month old, is induced to fetch a plastic brick. Luke has skills in, for example, holding an object in mind (working memory) and experiencing authorship (a feeling of conscious will). He can thus concentrate on the object while using maternal movements to link sucking, gaze-following, turn-taking, crawling and grasping. After the brick falls from Luke's mouth, nine seconds of focused attention give him time to anticipate that reward will accrue from fetching. As usual, the baby depends on both maternal micro-expression and how she acts to induce understanding. Strikingly, Luke uses the mother's manifest belief that he will be able to grasp what she wants him to do. On the slow time scale, Luke aligns to what she says (“*Do you want to fetch that?*”) by, smiling and crawling off to get the brick. The example is of a kind that often con-tributes to formats and, just as crucially, shows how caregiver movements enact a language stance. If a 'fetching game' develops, over-attributions may even prompt the mother to highlight sound-patterns (viz., “*fetch*”). The child thus becomes an intention reader across repetitions by, literally, using biomechanics to sense what can be done. Analysis-amenable behaviour emerges through the use of the other person's manifest goals.

According to this view, behaviour extends the form of co-action that emerged at three months. What has changed is that the child is now motivated to integrate self-implicating skills with capacities based in self-directed activity. As before, the baby exploits biomechanics that arose during its history of co-action with others. In short, children link their sense of persons with knowledge of what they can do with caregivers. The rise of this *triadic behaviour,* then, further extends grounded symbols. Infants link their doings to objects and real-time expression in ways that align what they do to verbal patterns: When asked to fetch the block, the baby fetches it. The approach proposed here is novel in providing an explanation that depends, not on appeal to wordings, but to the child's having learned to use situa-tions in self-regulating ways.

All agree that such events emerge at this stage and, equally, that they are im-portant in learning to talk. Where the distributed view diverges from others is in presenting this as independent of speech sounds, a lexicon, or words and referents. Nor is there any need for Tomasello's (1999) species-specific intention reading. Rather, a child's self-regulating powers depend on linking person perception with what objects afford. This, of course, is not to deny that sound patterns can mark sit-uations, events and, perhaps, objects. Indeed, in the following weeks, children may supplement (apparent) understanding with acts of utterance and pointing. Given role reversal (Tomasello, 1999, 2003) one-year-olds may make a “*more*” sound to ask for cake (in English-speaking settings) or use “*aah*” to show surprise. Once a baby is self-regulating, systematic use of sound patterns can bring many gains. While still relying on how inner symbols are extended, a caregiver's response to a baby's utterance-acts gives new information about how local norms constrain the situation. As the child gains experience of what to expect, vocalisations can be used more effectively. Eventually, it will learn to use them when referring to utterances made by both caregivers and its own *self* and, at this point, will be close to developing belief in *words*. Having used how caregivers integrate speech and action, aligning to verbal patterns will then reveal other levels of interactional structure. The helpless infant uses such tricks in gradually becoming a 'little person.'

The extended symbol hypothesis

Learning to talk depends on motivated actions which are integrated, in increasingly sophisticated ways, with norm-based expression. Thus, by the end of the first year, a child can align to a few sound patterns used by caregivers. This depends, I have argued, on a history of co-ordination that, by the fourth month, exploits the co-ordinated workings of two brains. According to this view, contingencies that link situations to brain-side events transform the child's agency. Learning to talk depends on how changing patterns of co-action extend the baby's already grounded symbols. This hypothesis can be summarised as follows:

1. Infants use biomechanics to exploit caregiver bodily movements that represent local norms (values, beliefs and practices).
2. Biomechanics link affect with caregiver expectations, beliefs and cultural values.
3. Caregivers attribute sense to the biomechanical output: given affect, these beliefs can shape future behaviour.
4. Infants integrate a practical grasp of local norms with what caregivers want and thus gain practical knowledge of situations.
5. Given dual control, just as the caregiver shapes the baby's strategic signals, the baby alters those of the caregiver.
6. A baby forms a motivation system; a caregiver uses its products to construct a baby's de facto understanding.

According to the extended symbol hypothesis (ESH), social development integrates growth and learning with the social events that forge infant agency. Given openness to culture and changing motivations, learning to talk is surprisingly transparent. The baby depends, above all, on the use of affect to discover cultural norms. Infants thus sensitise to situations in ways that exert leverage on adult doings. Gradually, as adult goals change, infants develop their agency and, after nine months, begin to align their doings to verbal patterns. Learning to talk thus emerges under dual control. It depends on a baby's changing motivations as well as how caregiver attributions are enacted in real-time. What adults hear as first *words* are, thus, based in how affect has shaped a history of co-actions that elicited manifest caregiver beliefs (and thoughts). For from being output from a neural system, these *words* constitute a new form of jointly regulated behaviour.

Beyond the symbol grounding problem

The SGP can be addressed by making invariant features of an environment relevant to action by symbol processing agents. While logical, this conceptualisation throws little light on the grounding of social symbols. Infants extend already-grounded symbols and, in so doing, have no need for speech sounds. Learning to talk, in other words, does not depend on grounding symbols in verbal forms. Rather, it is a consequence of how agency changes as infants become skilled in co-acting. Much thus depends on the caregiver's consistent use of the language stance. Thus while (inner) symbols are physically grounded, early *words* are situationally sensitive actions. Far from representing speech sounds to themselves, infants rely on biomechanics. Given that these shape motive formation the consequence is that infants gradually become self-regulating agents. Avoiding the hard task of grounding verbal forms, babies link experience to how caregivers enact attributions and beliefs. The extended symbol hypothesis thus has striking implications for language-using robots. It implies, above all, that expression can transform agency. Elsewhere, it is argued that attention be given to using multimodal action to simplify cognitive problems (Cowley & MacDorman, 2006). This raises the issue of whether robots can use learning to develop aspects of personhood (MacDorman & Cowley, 2006).

In human symbol grounding, co-action transforms agency. By 12 months, infants exploit situations to utter grounded wordings. Once children become self-regulating, they can use these wordings to develop new wants (or goals). For example, they may discover, as Luke had learned, that caregivers can be used to fetch items. This, however, depends on acting in self-regulating ways by using sound patterns that, broadly, make sense against another person's expectations. Eventually, using increasingly deliberate forms of action, children come to hear utterances as made up of recurrent patterns of units that can get things done. As the trick gets used, children begin to act as if they were users of a culturally evolved phonological system (Worgan & Damper, 2007). Later, their brains will enable them to develop mastery of constructions (Tomasello, 2003) while, in all likelihood, making use of mimetic schemas (Zlatev, 2002). Even after the first year, adult attitudes and beliefs will nudge children towards use of verbal patterns. Children, however, also learn new skills. Above all, an emergent ability to repeat what they and others say will, eventually, enable them to talk about talk (Taylor, 1997). In learning to hear words an infant acquires routines like saying *"What is that?"* As Vygotsky (1986) noted, a similar process occurs as self-directed speech gradually becomes silent rehearsal. Indeed, it is likely that developed forms of self-regulation use word-infected symbols as the basis for new powers of verbal imagination. This, moreover, fits Viger's (2007) appeal to an *acquired language of thought*. In contrast to the claims of code models, human language is grounded in the use of an emergent grasp of situations to control vocalisations. Symbol grounding allows culturally-evolved norms (and verbal patterns) to be used in forms of action that transform our cognitive powers.

Models and applications

The claim that babies gradually extend grounded symbols until they are heard to be speaking has many implications. First, it becomes important to separate evolutionary from epigenetic emergence because, implicitly, language and talk have different histories. Conceivably, while verbal patterns derive from cultural selection, these vehicles are of no importance to infants. Accordingly, while it makes sense to model the emergence of verbal (and phonological) patterns in populations, these units may be developmentally marginal. Those concerned with interaction, therefore, might gain much from building machines that use situations to alter their powers. In principle, machines too could use co-action to align to social norms (and, indirectly, words and values). According to this view of human symbol grounding, the roots of utterance acts lie, not in verbal patterns, but in the semantic properties of co-action. While the suggestion is, I think, novel, it is in line with much contemporary thinking. First, following Humphrey (1976), there is a wide consensus that human intelligence has a social basis which, for many, depends on something akin to an extended phenotype (e.g., Dawkins, 1982; Deacon, 1997; Laland, Odling-Smee & Feldman, 2000). Developing such views, Ross (2007) construes human signalling as unique in its capacity to impose structure on the world. This *digitality* draws on compressed cultural information that may appear, for example, in how a mother rebukes her child or a child's attempt to change her attentional focus. Similar lessons seem to be implied by Cangelosi's (2007) simulations which are said to show, for example, that 'verb' is not an abstract category. Rather, the term characterises signals that are "integrated with an agent's past history" in ways that shape behaviour. While emphasis on co-action is novel, one must ask if artificial agents could use cultural contingencies. This would link with the strategic emphasis of game theory and, specifically, the view that affect is the main currency of social interaction (Ross & Dumouchel, 2004). Indeed, in human symbol grounding, affect prompts babies to use cultural constraints. Culture is a supra-individual entity that, among other things, enables biological individuals to become people.

Infants neither possess nor learn quasi-verbal symbols. Rather, human symbol grounding depends on learning to act strategically in the social situation. Language functions, therefore, by enabling babies to develop into persons. Not only is this learning emphasis compatible with Turing (1950) but it fits Dennett's (1991) view of selves. Beyond this, it throws light on, say, the achievements of Alex the parrot (Pepperberg, 1999) and Kanzi the bonobo (Cowley & Spurrett, 2003; Savage-Rumbaugh et al., 1998). Both learn by integrating complex biomechanics with trainer use of the language stance. As a result, both become strikingly person-like. Could artificial agents use co-action to produce similar outcomes? This view of human symbol grounding thus suggests new issues for human-robot interaction and, above all, android science (MacDorman & Ishiguro, 2006a, 2006b). Stressing the importance of experience-prompted action,[10] Cowley and MacDorman (2006) propose that human micro-responding could, in principle, enable androids to discover social norms by using human displays of beliefs and values. The distributed view of language thus has striking consequences for robotics. Indeed, a system that mimicked babies would learn by connecting human expression to the world. Integrated intelligence (Seabra Lopes & Connell, 2001) could link material and semantic aspects of utterances. Indeed, by emphasising contingency, models of encounters become relevant to robotics. Such machines might encourage us to co-operate by acting to mimic how we respond to feelings (Cowley & Kanda, 2005).

Conclusion

Symbol grounding is inseparable from Chomsky's insight. Since human agents follow rules that can be formulated (not mindless distributional analysis), language is surely the source of productive, compositional and inference-bearing thought. Tying this to brain-centred models, Harnad (1990) argues that the underlying units are explicitly represented. In his formulation of the symbol grounding problem, therefore, the system maps real-word references onto the symbols on which rules operate. In seeking to naturalise the issue, I have accepted Harnad's view of how agents ground symbols into objects. In relation to learning to talk, however, the evidence suggests that the process proceeds quite differently. In human symbol grounding, I have suggested, infants have no need for explicitly represented linguistic forms (or *words*). Rather they rely on how caregiver construals enable them to develop strategies for acting — and vocalising — in response to situations. The symbols which ground objects are thus extended in ways that differ from those needed to ground 'linguistic forms.' While we learn about the physical world by interacting with objects, human expression and affect mediate our dealings with verbal patterns. Initially at least, babies learn to talk by using strategies that are parasitic on the caregiver's language stance.

Using Saussure's view of forms, Bloomfield, Harris, Chomsky and Harnad all accept the folk view that language is grounded in *words*. This, I have argued, is to confuse an analytic claim with an empirical one. Like other behaviour, language is based in action and perception. Specifically, as babies extend grounded symbols, verbal patterns emerge in co-action where the behaviour of both parties orients to local norms. Thus while formal models capture aspects of what the child masters, the resulting language knowledge differs from what analytical models describe. As Matthews (1967) argues in his review of *Aspects of the Theory of Syntax* (Chomsky, 1965), infants do not learn to talk by representing what formal models make explicit. Developing this view, I suggest that infants learn to talk by elaborating already-grounded symbols with respect to an expected response from a caregiver. Implicitly, the verbal patterns that shape what they do arise, not from a single process (e.g., natural selection, ontogenesis), but events that derive from several timescales. Far from explicitly representing verbal patterns, infants use expression as a basis for constructing *selves*. When Luke fetches the block, he aligns to what is said and, thus, enacts a semantic interpretation. In his world, he becomes a fetcher.

Far from solving the SGP, appeal to human symbol grounding shows the problem is more complex than previously thought. Indeed, if the extended symbol hypothesis is correct, those who examine language grounding have been looking in the wrong place. Human agents ground symbols into verbal patterns, not by categorising expression, but by prompting caregivers to make consistent use of the language stance. As motivated co-ordination develops, infants slowly develop into agents with the necessary powers. Just as to dance one need to become a dancer, to talk, one needs to become a talking agent. This peculiar capacity depends, on the one hand, on neural systems that shape motives and, on the other, on using affect to become sensitised to expectations. Since human infants are transformed by what situations (objects and people) afford, the grounding agent (a system) cannot be separated from the behaviour that is grounded (language). This claim has important implications for those who aim to develop semiotic models. It suggests that while agents need to become action guided perceivers, it is likely that, for brains, there can be no such thing as a pure symbol.[11] Words are *a posteriori* constructs that exist for a self-regulating agent who acts to draw on the doings and beliefs of others.

For modellers, the perspective poses the issue of how agents learn to exploit cultural constraints (especially nonverbal contingencies). Moreover, it posits that human infants use verbal patterns to shape co-occurring actions. According to the extended symbol hypothesis, however, words need never be explicitly represented.

Rather, co-action serves in discovering verbal patterns that, later, shape both inference-based reasoning and identity. Human subjects, then, are themselves the products of how expressive dynamics connect bodies with the verbal patterns of a cultural heritage. With Ross (2007), signals can function to repartition the world. We are unlike other primates in that we learn to adopt and alter perspectives on what is possible. The distributed view of language thus implies that population models need to explore how the (putatively) co-operative emergence of verbal patterns interacts with game theoretical models of human strategic signalling. The question, then, is whether we can build robots that use human co-action in ways that allow them to construct new levels of agency.

The extended symbol hypothesis has implications for epigenetic models. Given a Piagetian heritage, these often focus on how learning and growth shape interactions with a physically constrained world. Once language is viewed as a distributed meshwork, however, this seems unnecessarily narrow. Indeed, as argued above, much depends on how each party adjusts to the other both biomechanically and in the time domain of deliberate action. Inexperienced agents, I have claimed, unwittingly use this process to exploit culturally-structured events. By means of co-action they integrate aspects of social behaviour across several time scales. For robotics, if the ESH is broadly correct, many aspects of human agency or personhood may emerge as control systems integrate information from diverse sources. In other words to recognise a range of sound patterns as what we can write as *pferd,* we need neither phonological nor semantic categories. Rather the agent must be a self-regulator who has developed in a world where what English speakers call *horses* are salient during co-action.

Much can be gained from rethinking how infants extend the scope of already-developed (physically grounded) symbols. In seeking to develop more plausible views of child development, the two-stage model needs to be evaluated. Ideally, this will be done by robotic modelling. First, it needs to be shown that culturally constrained adult biomechanics can lead to significant changes in agency. In humans, then, one-year olds become agents who, occasionally, align their doings to verbal patterns. Second, we need to explore the view that the capacity develops as children come to act consistently with a language stance. They gain not only from acting as if they knew words but also talking about language (and linguistic knowledge). Humans need not learn natural languages because, oddly, it is enough to imagine that these systems are already known (in a community). A child becomes a person by coming to adopt the language stance. If this is plausible, the view has many consequences for human nature. Among other things, the extended symbol hypothesis offers new scope to models of how we can develop and sustain human kinds of autonomy.

Notes

* Among the many people who deserve thanks, I would like to give special thanks Karl F. Mac-Dorman who got me hooked on symbol grounding. Since then, I have to thank David Spurrett who kept the interest alive, Angelo Cangelosi who provided a way of linking up with a band of enthusiasts, and Tony Belpaeme who did the tough part of organizing ESG2006. Equally, I am very grateful to the participants who made the event worthwhile and the three anonymous referees who did their best to help me turn a rather unruly manuscript into a focused research paper.

1. This is the German equivalent of *horse*. I have chosen it to signal interest in grounding symbols into 'speech sounds' (or linguistic form). This may be harder than grounding them into *referents*.

2. Digital signals impose semantic structure on the world (Ross, 2007).

3. Not only are code models incompatible with empirical facts (Love, 2004, 2007), but they violate autopoietic principles (Kravchenko, 2004) and, for Ross (2007), presuppose an individualistic intelligence that is incompatible with natural selection.

4. Chomsky made a similar move by focusing on a *narrow* language faculty (Hauser, Chomsky and Fitch, 2002). As on the distributed view, this gives biomechanics a major role in the events of talk.

5. All behaviour is based in neural and bodily microdynamics. Their relevance to language is well illustrated by debate about when, to *some* ears, utterances of "gravy" sounded *unfriendly* (see, Eerdmans, Prevignano and Thibault, 2003). While some appeal to *contextualization cues*, Thibault (2003) treats this as showing the indexicality of language, and Cowley (2006b) claims that voice dynamics shape the feeling of what happens. The word *gravy* is just part of +/- 300ms of speech.

6. Paul Vogt picks this out as the remaining "non trivial" problem for his models. He puts it that there is currently no way of distinguishing utterances as forms from utterances as physical objects. On the view presented here, the baby depends exclusively on physical (not formal) properties of expression.

7. Trevarthen and Aitken (2001) give an overview of the neural systems used in intrinsic motive formation.

8. On a distributed view of language, children represent verbal patterns (off-line) only in talk about what is absent (typically, after age 3). Before then, circumstances prompt them to vocalise. Rather than using linguistic forms, they allow such patterns to constrain expression.

9. Those interested in modelling have given surprisingly little attention to social norms. Elsewhere Cowley and MacDorman (2006) argue both that the interaction order is crucial to humans and that, to deal with this, natural and social norms need to be brought into a single conceptual framework.

10. Following Kirsh and Maglio (1994), these "epistemic actions" contrast with actions that bring the agent closer to its goal.

11. Kravchenko (2007) notes that Peirce shares this view.

References

Anderson, M. L. (2003a). Embodied cognition. *Artificial Intelligence, 149*(1), 91–130.

Anderson, M. L. (2003b). Representations, symbols and embodiment. *Artificial Intelligence, 149*(1), 151–156.

Bloomfield, L. (1933). *Language*. George Allen & Unwin: London.

Bråten, S. (1988). Between dialogical mind and monologic reason: Postulating the virtual other. In M. Campanella (Ed.), *Between Rationality and Cognition*, pp. 205–236. Turin: Meynier.

Bruner, J. S. (1978). From communication to language. A psychological perspective, *Cognition, 3*, 255–287.

Brooks, R. A. (1999). *Cambrian intelligence: The early history of the new AI*. Cambridge, MA: MIT Press.

Campos, J. J. & Sternberg, C. (1981). Perception, appraisal, and emotion: The onset of social referencing. In M. E. Lamb & L. R. Sherrod (Eds.), *Infant social cognition: Empirical and theoretical considerations*, pp. 273–314. Hillsdale, NJ: Lawrence Erlbaum.

Cangelosi, A. (2006). The grounding and sharing of symbols. *Pragmatics and Cognition, 14*(2), 275–285.

Cangelosi, A. (2007). Adaptive agent modeling of distributed language: Investigations on the effects of cultural variation and internal action. *Language Sciences, 29*. 633–649.

Cangelosi, A. Greco, A. & Harnad, S. (2002). Symbol grounding and the symbolic theft hypothesis. In A. Cangelosi & D. Parisi (Eds.), *Simulating the evolution of language*, pp. 191–210. Springer: London.

Chomsky, N. (1965). *Aspects of the theory of syntax*. Cambridge, MA: MIT Press.

Clark, A. (1997). *Being there: Putting brain, body and world together again*. Cambridge, MA: MIT Press.

Cowley, S. J. (1997). Of representations and language. *Language and Communication, 17*(4), 279–300.

Cowley, S.J. (2003). Distributed cognition at three months: mother-infant dyads in kwaZulu-Natal. *Alternation*, 10(2), 229–257.

Cowley, S. J. (2004). Simulating others: The basis of human cognition? *Language Sciences, 26*(3), 273–299.

Cowley, S. J. (2006a). Distributed language: Biomechanics, functions and the origins of talk. In C. Lyon, C. L. Nehaniv & A. Cangelosi (Eds.), *Emergence of Communication and Language*, pp. 105–129. London: Springer.

Cowley, S. J. (2006b). Language and biosemiosis: A necessary unity? *Semiotica,* 162(1/4), 417–444.

Cowley, S. J. (2007). The cradle of language: making sense of bodily connexions. In D. Moyal-Sharrock (Ed.), *Perspicuous presentations: Essays on Wittgenstein's philosophy of psychology*, pp. 278–298. London: MacMillan Palgrave.

Cowley, S. J. & Spurrett, D. (2003). Putting apes, (body and language) together again. *Language Sciences, 25*(3), 289–318.

Cowley, S. J., Moodley, S. & Fiori-Cowley, A. (2004). Grounding signs of culture: Primary intersubjectivity in social semiosis. *Mind, Culture and Activity, 11*(2), 109–132.

Cowley, S. J & Kanda, H. (2005). Friendly machines: Interaction-oriented robots today and tomorrow. *Alternation, 12*(1), 79–106.

Cowley, S. J. & MacDorman, K. F. (2006). What baboons, babies and Tetris players tell us about interaction: A biosocial view of norm-based social learning. *Connection Science, 18*(3).

Davidson, D. (1986). A nice derangement of epitaphs. In E. LePore (Ed.), *Truth and interpretation*, pp. 433–446. Oxford: Blackwell.

Dawkins, R. (1982). *The extended phenotype: The long reach of the gene.* Oxford: Oxford University Press.

Deacon, T. (1997). *The symbolic species: Co-evolution of language and the brain.* London: Norton.

Dennett, D. (1991). The origins of selves. *Cogito, 3,* 163–173.

Donald, M. (1991). *Origins of the modern mind.* Cambridge, MA: Harvard University Press.

DeLanda, M. (1997). *A thousand years of nonlinear history.* New York: Zone Books.

Eerdmans, S. L., Prevignano, C. L. & Thibault, P. J. (2003). *Language and interaction.* Amsterdam: John Benjamins.

Halliday, M. A. C. & Matthiessen, C. (1999). *Construing experience through meaning: A language-based approach to cognition.* London: Cassell.

Harnad, S. (1990). The symbol grounding problem. *Physica D, 42,* 335–346.

Harris, Z. (1951). *Structural linguistics.* Chicago: Chicago University Press.

Hauser, M., Chomsky, N. & Fitch, T. (2002). The faculty of language: What is it, who has it and how did it evolve? *Science, 298,* 1569–1579.

Humphrey, N. (1976). The social function of intellect. In P. P. G. Bateson & R. Hinde (Eds.), *Growing points in ethology,* pp. 303–317. Cambridge: Cambridge University Press.

Jackendoff, R. (2002). *Foundations of language: Brain, meaning, grammar, evolution.* Oxford: Oxford University Press.

Karmiloff K. & Karmiloff-Smith A. (2001). *Pathways to language: From fetus to adolescent.* Cambridge, MA: Harvard University Press.

Kaye, K. (1982). *The mental and social life of babies: How parents create persons.* London: Methuen.

Kirsh, D. & Maglio, P. (1994). On distinguishing epistemic from pragmatic action. *Cognitive Science, 18,* 513–549.

Kravchenko, A. (2007). Essential properties of language, or, why language is not a code. *Language Sciences, 29.* 650–671.

Kugiumutzakis, G. (1999). Genesis and development of infant mimesis in early imitation of facial and vocal models. In J. Nadel & B. Butterworth (Eds.), *Imitation in infancy,* pp. 36–59. Cambridge: Cambridge University Press.

Lakoff, G. & Johnson, M. (1980). *Metaphors we live by.* Chicago: University of Chicago Press.

Laland, K. N., Odling-Smee, F. J. & Feldman, M. W. (2000). Niche construction, biological evolution and cultural change. *Behavioral and Brain Sciences, 23*(1), 131–175.

Legerstee, M. (2005). *Infants' sense of people: Precursors to a theory of mind.* Cambridge: Cambridge University Press.

Love, N. (2004). Cognition and the language myth. *Language Sciences, 26*(6), 525–544.

Love, N. (2007). Is language a digital code? *Language Sciences, 29.* 690–709.

MacDorman, K. F. (1999). Grounding symbols through sensorimotor integration. *Journal of the Robotics Society of Japan, 17*(1), 20–24.

MacDorman, K. F. & Ishiguro, H. (2006a). Toward social mechanisms of android science: A CogSci 2005 workshop. *Interaction Studies, 7*(2), 289–296.

MacDorman, K. F. & Ishiguro, H. (2006b). The uncanny advantage of using androids in cognitive and social science research. *Interaction Studies, 7*(3), 297–337.

MacDorman, K. F. & Cowley, S. J. (2006). Long-term relationships as a benchmark for robot personhood. *Proceedings of the 15th IEEE International Symposium on Robot and Human Interactive Communication.* September 6–9, 2006. University of Hertfordshire, Hatfield, UK.

Martinet, A. (Ed.). (1960). *Elements of general linguistics.* Chicago: University of Chicago Press.

Matthews, P. H. (1967). Review of Chomsky, N. *Aspects of the theory of syntax. Journal of Linguistics 3*(1), 119–152.

Matthews, P. H. (2001). *A short history of structural linguistics.* Cambridge: Cambridge University Press.

Meltzoff, A. N. & Moore, M. K. (1977). Imitation of facial and manual gestures by human neonates. *Science, 198,* pp. 75–78.

Oller, D. K. (2000). *The emergence of the speech capacity.* Mahwah, NJ: Lawrence Erlbaum.

Pattee, H. H. (2001). The physics of symbols: Bridging the epistemic cut. *Biosystems, 60,* 5–21.

Paul, H. (1891). *Principles of the history of language* (trans. H. A. Strong). London: Longmans Green.

Pepperberg, I. M. (1999). *The Alex studies: Cognitive and communicative abilities of grey parrots.* Cambridge, MA: Harvard University Press.

Pinker, S. (1994). *The language instinct: The new science of language and mind.* London: Penguin.

Port, R. F. & Leary, A. P. (2005). Against formal phonology. *Language, 81(4),* 927–964.

Ross, D. & Dumouchel, P. (2004). Emotions as strategic signals. *Rationality and Society, 16*(3), 251–286.

Ross, D. (2007). *H. Sapiens* as ecologically special: What does language contribute? *Language Sciences, 29.* 710–731.

Saussure, F. de (1916/1983). *Cours de linguistique générale.* [English translation by R. Harris.] London: Duckworth.

Savage-Rumbaugh, S., Shanker, S., & Taylor, T. J. (1998). *Apes, language and the human mind.* Oxford: Oxford University Press.

Seabra Lopes, L. & Connell, J. H. (2001). Semisentient robots: Routes to integrated intelligence. *IEEE Intelligent Systems, 16*(5), 10–14.

Seabra Lopes, L. & Chauhun, A. (2007). How many words can my robot learn? An approach and experiments with one-class learning. *Interaction Studies,* 8(1), 53–81.

Searle, J. (1980). Minds, brains, and programs. *Behavioral and Brain Sciences, 3,* 417–424.

Spurrett, D. & Cowley, S. J. (2004). How to do things without words: infants, utterance-activity and distributed cognition. *Language Sciences, 26*(5), 443–466.

Steels, L. & Belpaeme, T. (2005). Coordinating perceptually grounded categories through language. A case study for colour. *Behavioral and Brain Sciences, 28*(4), 469–489.

Stern, D. (1977). *The first relationship: Infant and mother.* London: Fontana.

Striano, T. & Rochat, P. (2000). Emergence of selective social referencing in infancy. *Infancy, 1*(2), 253–264.

Taddeo, M. & Floridi, L. (2005). Solving the symbol grounding problem: A critical review of fifteen years of research. *Journal of Experimental and Theoretical Artificial Intelligence. 17*(4), 419–445.

Taylor, T. J. (1997). *Theorizing language.* Oxford: Pergamon Press.

Thibault, P. J. (2003). Contextualization and social meaning-making practices. In S. Eerdmans, C. Prevignano & P. J. Thibault (Eds.), *Discussing John J. Gumperz,* pp. 41–61. Amsterdam: John Benjamins.

Tomasello, M. (1999). *The cultural origins of human cognition*. Cambridge, MA: Harvard University Press.

Tomasello, M. (2003). *Constructing a language: A usage-based theory of language acquisition* Cambridge MA: Harvard University Press.

Tønsberg, G H. & Hauge, T. S. (1996). The musical nature of prelinguistic interaction. The temporal structure and organization in co-created interaction with congenital deaf-blinds. *Nordic Journal of Music Therapy, 5*(2), 63–75.

Trevarthen, C. (1979). Communication and co-operation in early infancy: A description of primary intersubjectivity. In M. Bullowa (Ed.), *Before Speech*, pp. 321–347. Cambridge: Cambridge University Press.

Trevarthen, C. (1988). Universal co-operative motives: How infants begin to know the language and culture of their parents. In G. Jahoda & I. M. Lewis (Eds.), *Acquiring culture: Cross-cultural studies in child development,* pp. 37–89. London: Croom Helm.

Trevarthen, C. (1998). The concept and foundations of infant intersubjectivity. In S. Bråten (Ed.), *Intersubjective Communication in Early Ontogeny.* Cambridge: Cambridge University Press, pp. 15–46.

Trevarthen, C. & Aitken, K. J. (2001). Infant intersubjectivity: Research, theory and clinical applications. *Journal of Child Psychology and Psychiatry, 42*(1), 3–48.

Trevarthen, C. & Hubley, P. (1978). Secondary intersubjectivity: Confidence, confiding and acts of meaning in the first year. In A. Lock (Ed.), *Action, Gesture, and Symbol,* pp. 183–229. New York: Academic Press.

Turing, A. (1950). Computing machinery and intelligence. *Mind, 49,* 433–460.

Viger, C. (2007). The acquired language of thought hypothesis: A theory of symbol grounding. *Interaction Studies,* 8(1), 125–142.

Vogt, P. The physical symbol grounding problem. *Cognitive Systems Research Journal, 3*(3), 429–457.

Vygotsky, L. (1986). *Thought and Language*. [Trans. and Ed. A. Kozulin]. Cambridge, MA: MIT Press.

Wittgenstein, L. (1953). *Philosophical Investigations*. [Trans G. Anscombe]. Oxford: Blackwell.

Worgan, S. & Damper, R. (2007). Grounding symbols in the physics of speech communication. *Interaction Studies,* 8(1), 7–30.

Zlatev, J. (2002). Mimesis: The missing link between signals and symbols in phylogeny and ontogeny? In A. Pajunen (Ed.), *Mimesis, Sign and Language Evolution*, Publications in General Linguistics 3, University of Turku, Finland.

Semiotic symbols and the missing theory of thinking

Robert Clowes
Centre for Research in Cognitive Science, University of Sussex

This paper compares the nascent theory of the 'semiotic symbol' in cognitive science with its computational relative. It finds that the semiotic symbol as it is understood in recent practical and theoretical work does not have the resources to explain the role of symbols in cognition. In light of this argument, an alternative model of symbol internalisation, based on Vygotsky, is put forward which goes further in showing how symbols can go from playing intersubjective communicative roles to intrasubjective cognitive ones. Such a formalisation restores the symbol's cognitive and communicative dimensions to their proper roles.

Keywords: language and thought, symbol systems, semiotics, internalisation

Two kinds of symbol systems

Neuroscientist and author of *The Symbolic Species* (1997), Terrence Deacon, has argued that "there is probably no term in cognitive science more troublesome than the word 'symbol' " (2003, p. 117).[1] The problem, according to Deacon, hinges on two notions of the symbol that have been appropriated by different branches of the academy. The first notion is the computational (syntactic) account of symbols known from the Physical Symbol System Hypothesis (PPSH), and the second is the use of symbols as a means of understanding signification and referential systems, especially in language and other forms of communication. This second *semiotic* appreciation of the symbol is based on the analysis of systems of signs, and, in its modern forms, was developed in two different ways by the French linguist Ferdinand de Saussure and the American pragmatist philosopher Charles Sanders Peirce.

Deacon points out that while the two notions derive from the same intellectual tradition, their development has been such that there is today a deep rift in the conceptual schemes built around them. It may even be that the two notions are now, owing to their separate development, deeply incommensurable. Recent work in cognitive science has, however, suggested that the two notions may be combined or fused. This article will assess the present condition and future possibilities of such a fusion.

The first part of this paper introduces the two theoretical approaches to symbol systems. It then explores the latter *semiotic* approach to symbols in order to investigate what resources it has to explain the sorts of cognitive processes traditionally addressed by symbolically-minded cognitive science. Finding this account lacking, it then sketches a theoretical approach to how symbols developmentally reshape minds. The paper concludes by drawing attention to some future research directions for this vital but neglected area in cognitive science.

Physical symbol systems and cognition

The traditional cognitive science notion of what a symbol is, which we might call the *computational symbol,* is found in similar forms throughout the cognitive sciences[2] (especially linguistics, philosophy and psychology) and, as Deacon argues, also in mathematics. This notion of the symbol has at its heart the idea that it can support syntactically-based computational operations such as copying, deleting, substituting, and combining.

All of these operations happen according to formal rules with no regard, at base level, for semantics. This idea developed more or less simultaneously across several disciplines and the development of this *symbolic paradigm* offered unique resources to those thinking about cognition and promised to give an account of mind in purely formal terms. Indeed, it once seemed at least plausible that a complete account of cognition at the psychological level could be given in terms of a formal treatment of systems of symbols, their instantiation in physical processes and their manipulation according to systems of rules.

The main operationalization of the symbolic paradigm, called by Haugeland (1985) GOFAI (or Good Old Fashioned Artificial Intelligence) assumed cognitive architecture had to be understood in terms of symbols. With a theory of cognitive architecture organised around the symbol, it was hoped that a fully materialist account of the mind could be spelt out. Such a theory could make minds non-mysterious parts of the physical universe, and according to some, make psychology respectable.

The central reference point for the artificial intelligence understanding of a symbol is Newell and Simon's (1972) idea of a Physical Symbol System (PSS). According to Newel and Simon, the PSS hypothesis not only gave an account of how computational systems can solve well specified problems according to the purely syntactic manipulations of tokens, but it laid out the necessary and sufficient conditions for being an intelligent agent in terms of computational architecture. A PSS can be specified, according to Harnad, in terms of eight conditions. It must have (quoting Harnad):

1. a set of arbitrary "physical tokens" scratches on paper, holes on a tape, events in a digital computer, etc. that are
2. manipulated on the basis of "explicit rules" that are
3. likewise physical tokens and strings of tokens. The rule-governed symbol-token manipulation is based
4. purely on the shape of the symbol tokens (not their "meaning"), i.e., it is purely syntactic, and consists of
5. "rulefully combining" and recombining symbol tokens. There are
6. primitive atomic symbol tokens and
7. composite symbol-token strings. The entire system and all its parts — the atomic tokens, the composite tokens, the syntactic manipulations both actual and possible and the rules — are all
8. "semantically interpretable": The syntax can be systematically assigned a meaning, e.g., as standing for objects, as describing states of affairs (Harnad, 1990, p. 336).[3]

Fodor (1975; 1987) championed the theoretical justification of a symbol processing system as a theory of thinking principally to specify his computational Representational Theory of Mind (RTM). According to Fodor, a properly constituted theory of the role of symbols in cognition, or in his terminology, *Language of Thought* (or mentalese), is the foundation of a theory of thinking. He argued that tokens in the language of thought were processed in a syntactic manner that respects only their 'shape' or formal properties. A further role of the symbol in the RTM was to bind together two apparently very different types of property: the truth-preserving powers of reasoning and the intentional world-referring nature of thought.

Mental states were understood as relations to these physical symbols, and mental symbols were thought to have intrinsic representational powers, at least when embedded in the right sort of architecture. They also explained what we really mean when attributing propositional attitudes to other agents, such as in "Jones hopes that X," or "Mary believes that Y." Such propositional attitudes were essentially relations to mental symbols. So Jones was related by however his hope mechanisms are instantiated to the symbols encoding the Proposition X, and Mary by however her hope mechanisms are instantiated to symbols encoding Proposition Y. Symbols allowed us to explain both how reasoning happened and what mental states are.

An important implication was that mental states could thus be attributed to content, and play out inferential episodes of thought in a rational way that — according to Fodor — saved the central assumptions of folk psychology. Their representational powers accrued because of the powers of these internal symbols. As Fodor (1975) argued, "there is no internal representation without an internal language" (p. 55).[4] As Fodor makes clear, one of the chief benefits of this approach is that it reduces the problem of semantics to formal operations (Fodor, 2003).

Yet Fodor's notion of what it meant to have an internal language has proved profoundly unsatisfactory. As Fodor has himself admitted, there is little hope that the standard computational theory of symbols or anything much like it is going to explain the sorts of domain general cognition which the human mind seems to support so comprehensively (Fodor, 2000). And if it cannot give a good account of why human beings are rational, it becomes difficult to see the advantages of such a view.[5] Moreover, recent theories of cognition have made much of how the manipulation of symbols seems to be neither necessary nor sufficient for many properly cognitive episodes (Clark, 1997; Rowlands, 1999) and that much cognition is better conceived of as an entirely non-representational and situated engagement with the world (Brooks, 1991; Dreyfus, 2002). Such embodiment-based or *enactivist* approaches are the major challenger to cognitivism and have promised to give an account of cognition that makes no reference to symbols. Some cognitive scientists who would see themselves within a broadly embodimentalist tradition have, however, now started to question whether cognitive science could really do without the concept of the symbol.

Semiotic symbol systems

A series of theorists (Cangelosi, 2001; Deacon, 1997; Steels, 1999; Vogt, 2003) have recently adopted an alternative approach for understanding symbols. This has arisen in part as a way of dealing with some of the problems faced by the traditional computational symbol.[6] Its primary focus is to treat the representational abilities, first and foremost, of natural language and other derived and related *semiotic* systems and, in doing so, it is hoped, to show how a revived notion of symbol can once again play a central role in cognitive science. The theoretical background for the *semiotic* symbol which is most often invoked is taken from the work of the pragmatist philosopher Charles Sanders Peirce.

Peirce (1897) developed a formal theory of the sign in respect to its representational capacities, thus "a sign, or representamen, is something which stands to somebody for something in some respect or capacity" (Peirce, 1955, p. 99). He typologised the different kinds of reference that could be established in communication systems, which can be boiled down to the following:

Iconic — A relation of similarity or resemblance, so in the standard example a photograph represents something by virtue of looking like it. According to Deacon's gloss these simple relations can be understood as an over-generalisation of a learning mechanism.

Indexical — a relation of one-to-one reference or mapping, without similarity between indicator and referent. Sinha (1988) emphasizes how such indexical relations typically rely on causal connections, such as smoke indicating fire. The vervet monkey call-system can be regarded as a paradigmatic "natural" instance of an indexical communication system. (See Cheney & Seyfarth, 1992 for a detailed discussion of the vervet call system.)

Symbolic — A perceived relation between a sign, a referent and a concept or meaning mediated by conventionality (as explicated below). Because symbols do not generally stand in a one-to-one relationship with objects, an element of interpretation is always required.

The interpretational element of symbols is a complex issue. Sinha (2004, pp. 223–224) argues:

> The conventionality of a true symbol rests on the shared understanding by the communicating participants that the symbol is a token *representing* some referential class, and that the *particular* token represents a *particular* (aspect of) a shared situational context, and, ultimately, a shared universe of discourse. Conventional symbol systems are therefore *grounded* in an *intersubjective* meaning field in which speakers *represent*, through symbolic action, some segment or aspect of reality for hearers. This representational function is unique to symbolization, and is precisely what distinguishes a symbol from a signal. A signal can be regarded as a (possibly coded) *instruction to behave* in a certain way. A symbol, on the other hand directs and guides, not the behaviour of the organism(s) receiving the signal, but their *understanding* (construal) or (minimally) their *attention,* with respect to a shared referential situation.

Sinha emphasizes these complex interpretative aspects of the symbol to a much greater extent than Deacon and many other current cognitive-semiotic theorists who emphasise merely the proper instantiation of the internal triadic relationship of a symbol (also derived from Peirce's theory of signs). These allow us to decompose a symbol into its component relationships which can be most simply explained in terms of (Ogden & Richards, 1923) often reproduced semiotic triangle (Figure 1). According to this view, the symbol can be schematically reduced to a set of relationships among three elements: the representamen (or sign-vehicle), the object and the interpretant.[7]

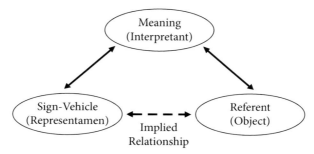

Figure 1. A semiotic triangle after (Ogden & Richards, 1923, p. 11).

Deacon's theoretical innovation was to give meaning to the semiotic symbol in terms of the implicit cognitive architecture that would be necessary to interpret the abstract relationships embedded in systems of properly symbolic signs. Whether a particular communication system is to be accorded the designation of symbolic is, however, a controversial matter. For the purposes of this discussion, I will define *minimal symbol users* as those who meet Deacon's criterion of having a cognitive architecture that can support the interpretation of conventional signs. Such minimal-symbol-users might be capable of only very impoverished symbol interpretation, according to Sinha's criterion. Nevertheless, minimal symbol users interpret signs which are embedded in a system of relationally-defined symbols. Such minimal symbol users can be found in simulation work such as the artificial agents found in Steels and Kaplan (1999) and Cangelosi, Greco and Harnad (2000).

It remains controversial, however, whether such minimal symbolic capabilities should be linked to the cognitive powers that traditional physical symbol systems are supposed to support. While the mechanics of semiotics might be of value in analysing communicative relationships, why should they be of any use in analysing cognition? In fact, attempts to work out the material basis to the formal relationships specified in Peirce's triad have formed the theoretical underpinning of some important recent projects which have attempted to explain symbol grounding and in doing so have gestured toward explaining some of the novel powers of human thought. While there are many such recent accounts, here I will focus on one project, *The Adaptive Language Games* (or ALG) project developed by Steels and his collaborators (Steels, 1999).

Can semiotic symbols play cognitive roles?

Paul Vogt's (2002) *The Physical Symbol Grounding Problem* is the most sustained attempt to show that the ALG framework can explain not only how symbols are grounded but also why they should still be regarded as a central concept in cognitive science. In this article Vogt implies that the semiotic symbol approach can solve the problems of symbolist cognitive science, or at least reduce them to "technical" problems by showing how symbols are grounded in communication.

Vogt's approach rests on solving the symbol grounding problem by proposing a rapprochement between embodied cognitive science and some elements of traditional cognitivism. He argues that symbolic structures can be used within the paradigm of embodied cognitive science by adopting an alternative definition of a symbol. In this alternative definition, the symbol may be viewed as a structural coupling between an agent's sensorimotor activations and its environment.

In Vogt's (2002) paper a robotic experiment is presented in which mobile robots develop a 'symbolic' structure from scratch by engaging in a series of language games. Through the language games, robots construct the means to refer to objects with a remarkable degree of success. Although the underlying meanings (interpretants) of a symbol may vary in different particular language games, agents eventually converge on a system of expressive forms (sign-vehicles) that allows them to pick out referents. That is, the community of agents converge on the same expressive means through communicational episodes, and these episodes in turn structure the agent's internal categorisation of the objects they encounter. The dynamics of the game allows a coherent system of semiotic symbols, in the minimal sense described above, to be developed. This is the basic (yet impressive) result that has been explored from the ALG perspective in a series of papers (Steels & Belpaeme, 2005; Steels & Kaplan, 1999). However, what is interesting for us here is whether these results bear on the question of the role of symbols in thinking.

Vogt develops the basic approach in a discussion of Brooks' earlier work on intelligence without representation (Brooks, 1991). Questioning Brooks' anti-symbolic stance, he asks rhetorically:

> But is it true? Are symbols no longer necessary? Indeed much can be explained without using symbolic descriptions, but most of these explanations only dealt with low-level reactive behaviours such as obstacle avoidance, phototaxis, simple forms of categorization and the like (Vogt, 2002, p. 430).

Several theorists (Clark & Grush, 1999; Clark & Toribio, 1994) have raised similar questions. Vogt's preferred solution to the problem comes from a re-interpretation of the symbol along embodimentalist lines. He argues that to overcome the symbol grounding problem, the symbol system has to be embodied and situated. Brooks' *physical ground hypothesis* states "that intelligence should be grounded in the interaction between a physical agent and its environment. Furthermore, according to this hypothesis, symbolic representations are no longer necessary. Intelligent behaviour can be established by parallel operating sensorimotor couplings" (2002, p. 432). Moreover, the way to accommodate symbols in the new situated-embodied perspective is to view them as structural couplings, using Maturana and Varela's

(1970) concept. Such an approach is perhaps a reasonable theoretical direction from which one might attempt to subsume symbols into the embodied systems perspective, but is does beg the question of exactly what type of structural coupling they are.

Vogt argues that "when symbols should be necessary to describe cognition, they should be defined as structural couplings connecting objects to their categories based on their sensorimotor projections" (2002, p. 432). This definition, Vogt notes, echoes Peirce's view. Vogt goes on to present something like a standard theory of internal representation with an embodimentalist twist:

> Each interaction between an agent and a referent can activate its past experiences bringing forth a new experience. The way these bodily experiences are represented and memorized form the internal representation of the meaning. The actual interaction between an agent and a 'referent' defines the functional relation (2002, p. 434).

But it seems the "symbols" so established are just associations between internal sense and external reference and are constituted simply by establishing the right sort of association. Such an associationist refiguring of the symbol, however, gives us no way of understanding the difference between the symbolic mode of structural coupling and any other type of structural coupling, and raises the suspicion that what is going on is the formal re-defining of an association as a symbol.[8]

The missing theory of thinking

The ALG approach promises a unification of several dimensions of cognitive science theory. It holds the possibility of providing a mechanistic account of a series of seemingly mysterious processes: how languages are born, how they are maintained, how agents can coordinate categories, and how cultural categories can come into being and be shared across generations.

At first sight it would seem that proposing answers to these questions should open doors to understanding the cognitive role of language. Nevertheless, in examining the ALG approach, it is clear that "symbols" generated in this way cannot be shown, in a straightforward way, to support traditional cognitive properties. The ALG approach is typically constituted to insulate language from forms of cognitive activity other than categorisation. Despite its argument that language is central to our cognitive adaptivity, the ALG approach actually fixes everything other than the content of the categories in the agent's architecture.

What is lacking is any sense of how such semiotic symbols play a role in cognitive episodes beyond the picking out of referents in scenes; this is the main task for the agents in all ALG-type experiments. What appears to be missing is the sense that symbols play any role in inferencing or organising non-linguistic behaviour. The worry is that semiotic symbols have come unmoored from cognitive symbols and that therefore our theorising about communicative capacities has come unmoored from our theorising about cognition. But wasn't this link precisely what the semiotic symbol approach was supposed to theorise?

Perhaps there is much greater indebtedness than would first seem to be in the ALG approach to the GOFAI framework. Although there is no explicit defence of the idea in Steels' work, there is still a ghost of GOFAI in the assumption that in grounding symbols — via the components of the ALG — we can show that symbols also support other cognitive properties. While the ALGs provide architecture for linguistically grounding categories, they make no mention of how such architecture can help an agent to perform other cognitive work. This work seems to be silent on the question of how a symbol system, language system, system of external representations, or system of tools can play a role in reorganising underlying cognitive activity. (For a recent review of the importance of the consideration of this relationship, see Clark, 2006a)

Steels does acknowledge this problem in an article in which he states that the ALGs tell "only the first part of the story. What we still need to show is how these external representations may lead to the significant bootstrapping effect that we see in human development, where representations (drawings, language, pretend play) are a primary motor of cognitive development" (Steels, 2003, p. 14). This is just right but the central problem remains of how to theorise this process.

The semiotic view of the symbol offers a way in which the symbol grounding problem can be solved by offering a materialist explanation of how the dimensions of signifier and signified, or alternatively Peirce's triad of representamen, interpretant and object, could come into relation. It does this by spelling out what it is, at least minimally, for an agent to entertain a symbol and then showing how this can be cashed out in agent-based simulations. But unless some account of how cognitive architecture can emerge from its ability to interpret symbols is given, a theory of semiotic symbols will never be a serious challenger to GOFAI. The danger of declaring that the symbol grounding problem has been reduced to a technical problem is that it blinds us to the question of the role of semiotic symbols in cognition.

For rationalist and computational accounts of symbol systems, the role of the symbol is to allow inferencing; in essence, an idealisation of thinking shorn of its roots in the ongoing activity of the agent. But if semiotic symbols are held to play inferential or any other type of cognitive roles there must be some theory of how this happens. There appears to be a hidden assumption in Vogt's work on semiotic symbols to the effect that if it can be shown that symbols are grounded, then it can be shown that symbols support truly cognitive properties. But this does not follow. A theory of reference and signification is not a theory of inferencing.

If semiotic symbols are to factor into our accounts of cognition, they face a problem which is every bit as grave as the symbol grounding problem. Although this problem has attracted much less attention than the symbol grounding problem has, it might be dubbed the new problem of symbols. *How do semiotic symbols come to play a role in thinking?*

In what follows I will schematically develop what is needed. This explication will refer to some cognitive modelling work previously reported in Clowes and Morse (2005) that allows us to elaborate on the unique role of symbols in cognition, but it requires attention to how symbols are taken up to do cognitive work. The approach is based on Vygotsky's notion of *semiotic internalisation*.

Restructuring cognitive architecture through symbol internalisation

Here I present a hypothesis of how developing systems can restructure themselves through the internalisation of symbols. This hypothesis both helps us make sense of some previously reported simulation-based experiments (Clowes & Morse, 2005) and shows how this work may be linked to Vygotsky's theory of the establishment of higher-cognitive functions (Vygotsky, 1997). Our simulation-based experiments contained agents, embedded in a dynamic environment in which objects could be moved around. Agents were evolved to move objects to target locations within the environment in line with signalled instructions. The neural architecture of the agents was such that they could adapt to re-trigger their own signal reception mechanisms. In these simulations agents came to re-use this re-triggering mechanism to control their own ongoing activity and perform self-regulative functions. Below I argue that this kind of self-regulative function explain the proper cognitive character of the symbol.

According to the following analysis, I argue that we can schematise the three stages of reorganisation that an agent must go through as it internalises symbols:

1. Completing a symbolically initiated action
2. Stabilising activity with symbols
3. Establishing activity regulation with symbols

Completing a symbolically initiated action

If we assume that children are not born knowing what symbols are or how to use them,[9] we have to assume that they learn about symbols in action. Such a hypothesis requires an *outside-in* understanding of the trajectory of symbols and their role in the regulation and production of behaviour.

However, we certainly should not assume that just because a child can respond appropriately to the use of a symbol that he or she has a fully developed command of symbol interpretation. Vygotsky's colleague Luria (1961) described a mother and child who were playing a game. The mother asks the child, "Where is Lenin?", and the child, having played the game before, points to a painting of Lenin on the wall. Next, the painting of Lenin is moved and the mother asks again "where is Lenin?" The child points at the place where the picture had hung.

The message should be clear. It is possible for the developing child to have an incredibly imperfect grasp of the thoughts and activities that adults can structure around symbols, and yet no understanding of the deeper interpretative relationships at work. Yet the child is immersed in a world of symbols and some of the most basic interactions with which the child will learn about the world are, from the very first moment, symbolically structured.

In our simulations, agents are confronted with a similar task: to complete an activity sequence which was initiated symbolically from without. As just discussed, this does not mean that the agent needs to understand the meaning of the symbol, if by "understand" we mean some high-level conceptual ability. Our simple simulated agents have no such capacities. However, within acceptable criteria, the agent can interpret the symbol in accordance with the expectations of the speech community from which the symbol has been introduced. The first behavioural regime the agent must go through is the establishment of a behaviour, or group of behaviours (or cognitions) with respect to an instruction, or other form of speech act. We call this the stage of *minimal symbol interpretation*.

Figure 2 shows the agent embedded in a series of ongoing interactions (the large curving arrows). The arrows form a rough circle show that these agents are engaged in a continual dynamic interaction with their environment.

In the diagram, some of these interactions are singled out for special attention. These are the externally generated 'words' that the agents must interpret, and are shown as square speech bubbles with arrows at the bottom of the diagram. To operate as symbols even in the most minimal sense, these words must be interpreted. Interpretation, at least in this base level language game requires an action. The diagram depicts the neural aspects of these interpretations as thought bubbles, but this is somewhat misleading. Interpretations here really consist of activities, for example, moving objects around in the world. These dynamic interactions with the environment accomplish much of the information processing, or *cognitive* work, of an active perception system, which need not be interpreted as relying on exhaustive representational systems (Clark, 1997).

This schematic account of the first stage of symbol internalisation merely requires that an agent be able to complete, in the required way, a symbolically-

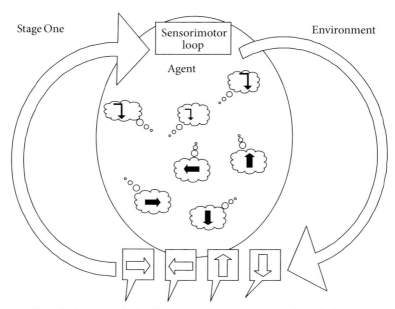

Figure 2. Completing a symbolically initiated action (minimal symbol interpretation).

initiated action. One might object that the kind of closely coupled action systems that Luria observed between child and mother could just as well be described as a loosely coupled action system with no real initiator. We could simply consider the mother and child as continually completing, regulating and adapting to each other's activities as in an intimate dance (Cowley, 2007). Yet while the developing relationship between mother and child is built on a whole series of such interactions, the mother initiates their *symbolic character* (as Cowley also recognises). The earliest *symbolically*-initiated actions are when the child completes the mother's action and are thus, as Vygotsky argued, outside-in. It is because symbols first appear for children in such intimate encounters and are only later taken-up by the developing child to structure its own activities that we should understand the process of symbolic development as one of *internalisation*.

Stabilising activity with symbols

Words are generally embedded in a series of affective regulation systems that support the construction of activities (Cowley, 2007; Trevarthen, 1991) and are often used to initiate activities from the outside. Typically, these sorts of affective interactions between mother and child provide a series of tacit supports and scaffolds to the child's developing activity system (Bruner, 1983). A whole series of largely unconscious mechanisms seems to be at work in establishing some very basic social psychological functions, such as triadic interactions (Leavens, 2006). In addition, of course, there are some very conscious interactions, as the mother seeks to engage her child in aspects of the surrounding world.

Yet in the midst of these developing interaction systems, the child also faces a problem. If symbolic regulation is to play a role in structuring the child's own autonomous activities, *symbols must be wrested from their public source and appropriated for self-directed activity*. Appropriation of symbols requires performance without some of those social scaffolds. Accomplishing this task seems to require the development of internal mechanisms which can take over the role of some of these supports.

Vygotsky discussed similar problems in his writings on the question of the differentiation of functions of egocentric speech (Vygotsky, 1986). As egocentric speech develops towards properly self-regulative internal-speech, there is developmental evidence that the child has difficulty in wresting this speech from its social source. Vygotsky writes, "in the process of growth the child's social speech, which is multifunctional, develops in accordance with the principle of the differentiation of separate functions, and at a certain age it is quite sharply differentiated into egocentric and communicative speech" (cited in Wertsch, 1985, p. 117). In the first stages of the development of using self-directed speech for control, as Wertsch notes, Vygotsky "reasoned that one should find a lack of differentiation or even thorough confusion between social and egocentric speech in young children's verbal behaviour" (Wertsch, 1985, p. 118).

Vygotsky empirically tested this hypothesis of progressive differentiation with three experiments, each of which was designed to test the child's ability to differentiate social from egocentric speech in action. Egocentric speech, according to Vygotsky, is by definition involved in self-control functions. Yet social contact was found to regulate the production of egocentric speech in a variety of experimental conditions. Children use much less egocentric speech in situations where they have less chance of being understood by others. Vygotsky explained this as an initial difficulty with differentiating social from self-organisational functions.

Vygotsky frames the problem in terms of how a child has to learn to use self-directed speech in the absence of adults or other children. This is difficult because speech must be turned from its social function. The problem of gaining control of these minimally-symbolic interpretation systems is also a problem for the agents in our simulations (Clowes & Morse, 2005). This problem confronts the agents in a number of forms.

First, there is simply the problem of developing and using a self-directed loop. In our simulations, agents have the capacity to trigger themselves because of their re-entrant architecture. However they initially switch this off because self-triggering interferes with their capacity to interpret signals generated from outside. Self-generated signals may be mistaken for external ones and upset the developing activity pattern. To take advantage of self-generated signals, agents must learn to differentiate those that are self-generated from those that emanate from outside. The problem of appropriating symbols to self-control manifests itself in the agent simulations. As reported in Clowes and Morse, early generation agents tend to turn off their internal loops until initial control regimes are stabilised. When they turn the loop back on at a more advanced stage, there is some initial drop in performance.

This is essentially a problem of self-organisation. The agent has developed interpretations, responses and structural couplings that are cued by "good" information, that is, information that the agent needs to achieve its goals. The advent of self-directed signals requires the restructuring of an agent's interpretation mechanisms as these can destabilise behaviour. Such potential for destabilisation predicts a U-shaped curve in developmental episodes when self-signalling becomes involved in self-regulation activity. However, regimes of self-stimulation begin to make new modes of self-regulating activity possible. At this point, the agent's self-stimulating use of its own interpretation mechanisms reflects more of a potential for activity than an actual new organisational regime of activity.

Figure 3 represents this transitional stage of development by showing a series of internally-generated speech bubbles that can trigger interpretation processes,

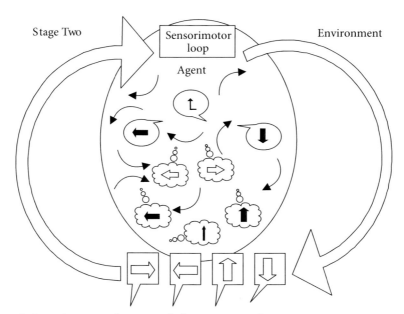

Figure 3. Learning to produce a symbol as a cue to action.

and which can in turn trigger the production of internally-generated "speech," (hence the internal partial loops shown by the small curved arrows). This stage of development implies a second type of cognitive architecture that develops as the agent starts to use symbols to stabilise its activities. This phase of activity re-ordering can begin once some symbol interpretation systems are in place. The establishment of action-based interpretation systems form a new platform on which the agent constructs new modes of action and self-regulation.

This stage of development is an unstable and transitional point as most of the agent's self-directed signals can be regarded as noise, but noise that has the potential to become a new kind of self-directed activity. In this phase the agent is faced with both problems and opportunities. As self-generated auto-stimulation loops become stabilised, the agent has the possibility of organising its activities according to new means of control that are established at a higher, semiotically generated, order of abstraction.

Establishing activity regulation with symbols

In this third stage, agent organisation has gone beyond the simple need to establish when an "utterance" comes from outside and when it is produced internally. It has therefore differentiated for itself *in practice* inside and outside. This differentiation allows new types of functional differentiation to take place. Now the agent is in a position to capitalise on these newly developed internally-directed speech circuit loops and to develop entirely new modes of activity. To do this, it needs to establish when auto-stimulation with words is useful and when it is unnecessary. In a sense, it needs to establish mastery of the sensorimotor contingencies of its own activity system.[10] As Vygotsky pointed out, this sort of development requires the progressive differentiation of functional systems that respond to externally-generated activity from those that respond to internally-generated activity.

In Figure 4, this is represented by the development of a new, functionally differentiated and *internal* activity loop. Unlike in the previous control regime, internally-generated loops do not simply capitalise on externally-generated and supported activity systems, but they develop new activity systems. The functional organisation of the activity of an individual agent has a logic that is not simply a recapitulation of the logic of the group. Public systems of representation produced socially are thereby turned to the agent's own ends. This point of development could be regarded as the point of completion of symbol internalisation, for the agent has now built a new mode of symbolically-mediated self-regulation that is essential to its ongoing activity.

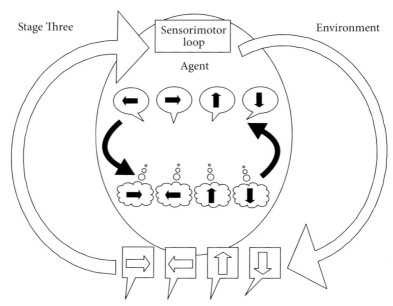

Figure 4. Establishing activity regulation with symbols.

Towards an understanding of semiosis in cognition

The theoretical model presented here and the experimental results presented in Clowes and Morse (2005) give us the beginnings of an account of how the internalisation of symbols come to reshape neural-dynamics. In contrast to other accounts of semiotic symbols systems, these models illuminate the neglected cognitive side of the semiotic symbol.

At a technical level, these models indicate one manner in which using external symbols can reorganise the basic mechanics of regulating activity in a minimal cognitive model. (Work is ongoing to understand this process in more detail.) At a more abstract level, they give us a sense of how activities and the structural couplings between agents and their environments can be stabilised around the concrete anchors made available by semiotic systems. Nevertheless, there is much work to do. This account represents only the beginnings of an understanding of how symbol internalisation reorganises cognition in human beings. To deepen this understanding we need to tackle the following questions:

1. How do words, and the external social representational systems in which they are embedded make available the contingencies through which agents restructure themselves?

2. What forces are at play in the internal dynamics of agents such that they can appropriate these structures?
3. How do the external and internal systems interact in the ongoing restructuring of agents?

The outside-in model forces us to treat explicitly how the representational structure of language allows an agent to shape its own cognitive architecture. I have argued for the need to understand this process through a sequence of functional changes. The first is how scaffolding (Bruner, 1983) gives way to semiotically-mediated joint control (Cowley, 2007) and how this in turn gives way to semiotically-mediated self-control (as Vygotsky emphasized). This process has profound implications for the attentional systems of the developing child, its sense of self and its agency; to understand this we need research on the unfolding functional changes that underpin internalisation.

Acknowledgments

The simulation work described above was carried out in association with Anthony Morse, and Sean Bell originally produced the diagrams. This paper has also benefited from the criticism of a panel of anonymous referees and much helpful advice from the special edition editors to whom I would like to express my thanks.

Notes

1. Whereas this is an accurate summary of today's state of affairs, we should add that the notion of symbol has become vastly more problematic as traditional GOFAI approaches to cognitive science have fallen into disfavour. The symbol has become a problem insofar as the more general research programme has become increasingly problematic.

2. The symbols which we find in AI, the philosophy of cognitive science and the generativist tradition in linguistics, which sees the formation of sentences as formal manipulations of syntax, share much in common. They are not, however, identical notions, and there is a nice discussion of some of the subtle differences between them in Chapter 7 of (Rowlands, 1999).

3. I cited at length from Harnad here because his view seems to be a fairly canonical one about what symbols are in the cognitive science community, even if there is not wide agreement on whether his view on how symbols are grounded is correct.

4. A curious upshot of this idea in its classical form is that language is a subsidiary phenomenon only made meaningful when it is translated into an inner language.

5. This is, of course, to leave aside the attendant problems of the seemingly unavoidable commitment to conceptual nativism (Fodor, 1998).

6. Actually, proposals for incorporating semiotic theory into the understanding of cognitive organisation have some longstanding proponents (Sinha, 1988). Perhaps the recent resurgence of interest in this area can be linked to the development of new techniques for modelling multi-agent systems, some of which are discussed below.

7. The original terminology used by Peirce in characterising the triadic relationship was *representamen, interpretant* and *object*. Vogt, Steels and his colleagues tend to use the terms *form* (or *word-form*), *meaning* and *referent* (Vogt, 2003). I prefer to refer to the representamen as *sign-vehicle* as this emphasises its role in conveying meaning.

8. In fact, if the main idea behind the semiotic conception of symbols is correct, properly the identification of a symbolic relationship would be a difficult task to perform at the level of the individual structural coupling of an agent and its environment. This is because the right sorts of structural couplings are not defined by the individual relationships, but by the *system* of relationships in which they are embedded. Vogt's attempted definition is at the very least missing a crucial feature.

9. As a number of theorists have argued, for example, (Clark, 2006b; Cowley, 2005; Sinha, 1988; Vygotsky, 1986).

10. This use of terminology is a gesture toward the theorisation of active perception developed in (O'Regan & Noë, 2001).

References

Brooks, R. (1991). Intelligence without representation. *Artificial Intelligence*(47), 139–160.

Bruner, J. S. (1983). *Child's talk*. Oxford: Oxford University Press.

Cangelosi, A. (2001). Evolution of communication and language using signals, symbols, and words. *IEEE Transactions on Evolutionary Computation, 5*(2), 93–101.

Cangelosi, A., Greco, A., & Harnad, S. (2000). From robotic toil to symbolic theft: Grounding transfer from entry-level to higher-level categories. *Connection Science, 12*(2), 143–162.

Cheney, D. L., & Seyfarth, R. M. (1992). Précis of *How monkeys see the world. Behavioral and Brain Sciences, 15*(1), 135–182.

Clark, A. (1997). *Being there: Putting brain, body, and world together again*. Cambridge, MA: MIT Press.

Clark, A. (2006a). Language, embodiment, and the cognitive niche. *Trends in Cognitive Sciences, 10*(8), 370–374.

Clark, A. (2006b). Material symbols. *Philosophical Psychology, 19*(3), 291–307.

Clark, A., & Grush, R. (1999). Towards a cognitive robotics. *Adaptive Behavior, 7*(1), 5–16.

Clark, A., & Toribio, A. J. (1994). Doing without representing. *Synthese, 10*, 401–431.

Clowes, R. W., & Morse, A. (2005). Scaffolding cognition with words. In L. Berthouze, F. Kaplan, H. Kozima, Y. Yano, J. Konczak, G. Metta, J. Nadel, G. Sandini, G. Stojanov & C. Balkenius (Eds.), *Proceedings of the 5th International Workshop on Epigenetic Robotics*. Nara, Japan: Lund University Cognitive Studies, 123. Lund: LUCS.

Cowley, S. J. (2007). How infants deal with symbol grounding. *Interaction Studies 8*(1), page-page.

Deacon, T. W. (1997). *The symbolic species: The co-evolution of language and the human brain*. London: Penguin.

Deacon, T. W. (2003). Universal Grammar and semiotic constraints. In M. H. Christiansen & S. Kirby (Eds.), *Language evolution: The states of the art*: Oxford University Press.

Dreyfus, H. L. (2002). Intelligence without representation. *Phenomenology and Cognitive Science, 1*(4), 367–383.

Fodor, J. (1975). *The language of thought*. New York: MIT Press.

Fodor, J. (1987). *Psychosemantics*: MIT Press.

Fodor, J. (1998). *Concepts: Where cognitive science went wrong. The 1996 John Locke Lectures*. Oxford: Oxford University Press.

Fodor, J. (2000). *The mind doesn't work that way: The scope and limits of computational psychology*. Cambridge MA: MIT Press.

Fodor, J. (2003, 9 October). More peanuts: Review of José Luis Bermúdez *Thinking without words*. *London Review of Books*.

Harnad, S. (1990). The symbol grounding problem. *Physica D, 42*, 335–346.

Haugeland, J. (1985). *Artificial intelligence: The very idea*. Cambridge, MA: MIT Press.

Leavens, D. A. (2006). It takes time and experience to learn how to interpret gaze in mentalistic terms. *Infant and Child Development, 9*, 187–190.

Luria, A. R. (1961). *The role of speech in the regulation of normal and abnormal behavior*. New York: Pergamon Press.

Maturana, H. R., & Varela, F. J. (1970). *Autopoiesis and cognition: The realization of the living*. Dordrecht: Reidel.

Newell, A., & Simon, H. A. (1972). *Human problem solving*: Englewood Cliffs, NJ: Prentice-Hall.

Ogden, C. K., & Richards, I. A. (1923). *The meaning of meaning: A study of the influence of language upon thought and the science of symbolism.* London: Routledge.

O'Regan, J. K., & Noë, A. (2001). A sensorimotor account of vision and visual consciousness. *Behavioral and Brain Sciences, 24*(5), 939–1011.

Peirce, C. S. (1955). *Philosophical writings of Peirce*. New York: Dover.

Peirce, C. S. (Ed.). (1897). *Logic as semiotic: The Theory of Signs* (1985 ed.). Bloomington, IN: Indiana University Press.

Rowlands, M. (1999). *The body In mind: Understanding cognitive processes*. Cambridge: Cambridge University Press.

Sinha, C. (1988). *Language and representation: A socio-naturalistic approach to human development*. London: Harvester.

Sinha, C. (2004). The evolution of language: From signals to symbols to system. In D. Kimgrough Oller & U. Griebel (Eds.), *Evolution of communication systems: A comparative approach* (pp. 217–237). Cambridge, MA: MIT Press.

Steels, L. (1999). *The talking heads experiment: Volume I. Words and meanings* (Pre-Edition ed.). Antwerpen: Laboratorium.

Steels, L. (2003). Intelligence with representation. *Philosophical Transactions: Mathematical, Physical and Engineering Sciences, 361*(1811).

Steels, L., & Belpaeme, T. (2005). Coordinating perceptually grounded categories through language: A case study for colour. *Behavioral and Brain Sciences, 28*(4), 469–489.

Steels, L., & Kaplan, F. (1999). Collective learning and semiotic dynamics. In D. Floreano, J. D. Nicoud & F. Mondada (Eds.), *Advances in artificial life (ECAL 99), Lecture Notes in Artificial Intelligence* (pp. 679–688). Berlin: Springer.

Trevarthen, C. (1991). The function of emotions in early infant communications and development. In J. Nadel & L. Camaioni (Eds.), *New perspectives in early infant communication and development* (pp. 48–81). London: Routledge.

Vogt, P. (2002). The physical symbol grounding problem. *Cognitive Systems Research, 3*(3), 429–457.

Vogt, P. (2003). Anchoring of semiotic symbols. *Robotics and Autonomous Systems, 43*(2), 109–120.

Vygotsky, L. S. (1986). *Thought and language* (7th ed.). Cambridge, MA: MIT Press.

Vygotsky, L. S. (1997). The history and development of higher psychological functions. In R. W. Rieber (Ed.), *The collected works of L. S. Vygotsky* (Vol. 4). New York: Plenum.

Wertsch, J. V. (1985). *Vygotsky and the Social Formation of Mind*. Cambridge, MA: Harvard University Press.

The acquired language of thought hypothesis

A theory of symbol grounding

Christopher Viger
Department of Philosophy, University of Western Ontario

I present the symbol grounding problem in the larger context of a materialist theory of content and then present two problems for causal, teleo-functional accounts of content. This leads to a distinction between two kinds of mental representations: presentations and symbols; only the latter are cognitive. Based on Milner's and Goodale's dual route model of vision, I posit the existence of precise interfaces between cognitive systems that are activated during object recognition. Interfaces are constructed as a child learns, and is taught, how to interact with her environment; hence, interface structure has a social determinant essential for symbol grounding. Symbols are encoded in the brain to exploit these interfaces, by having projections to the interfaces that are activated by what the symbols stand for. I conclude by situating my proposal in the context of Harnad's (1990) solution to the symbol grounding problem and responding to three standard objections.

Keywords: acquired language of thought hypothesis, content, dual route model of vision, interface, language of thought, presentation, representation, symbol, symbol system

Introduction

In posing the symbol grounding problem, Harnad (1990) put a new twist on the old problem of accounting for intentionality or meaning within a materialist framework, a problem posed by the scholastic philosophers and reintroduced in its modern form by Brentano (1874/1973). Very simply, materialism can only account for mental content by appealing to material objects and the relations in which they stand. How then can a materialist account for our thoughts about absent, abstract, or fictitious things[1] to which we either do not or cannot stand in any material relation? There seem to be no resources left for the materialist.

Behaviourism and eliminativism are materialist ways of eschewing the mental and thereby avoiding the problem; but because they avoid the issue rather than respond to it, they are unsatisfactory accounts of our mental life. There is, however, a way out for the materialist. The representational theory of mind (RTM), according to which mental representations are physical particulars, likely neural structures, is a materialist theory that offers a solution to Brentano's problem. We can have thoughts about unicorns or justice because we have a mental representation whose content is *unicornhood* or *justice*,[2] which is activated when we are thinking about unicorns or justice. The computational theory of mind (CTM) supplements RTM. According to CTM, thinking is similar to a computer performing syntactic transformations of representations that nonetheless preserve their semantic properties, such as truth.

RTM and CTM together offer a materialist solution to Brentano's problem, provided we can give a naturalistic explanation of the content of mental representations. So with RTM and CTM, Brentano's problem is transformed into the seemingly more tractable problem of giving a naturalistic account of mental content, though this is not yet the symbol grounding problem Harnad posed. Attempted solutions to naturalise content tend to be causal or teleo-functional accounts.[3] The effort in forming these accounts goes into finding some physical relation that a mental representation can stand in with just its extension, such as finding a relation between the symbol DOG and all and only dogs. Surprisingly, there is no discussion of how a creature activating a mental representation can be aware of the suggested relation. Harnad's new twist[4] is to note that it is not a theory of content *tout court* that is required, but rather a theory according to which symbols are meaningful for the creatures that use them. If the proposed relation between a mental representation and its extension is not one to which the creature is sensitive, then any instantiation of that relation is irrelevant to the creature and therefore fails to explain the content of its thoughts.

I present two problems for causal, teleo-functional accounts of content as they have been presented, which motivates a distinction between two kinds of mental representations, presentations and symbols, of which only the latter is cognitive. Based on Milner's and Goodale's dual route model of vision, I suggest a cognitive architecture that explains how symbols could be encoded in the brain so as to be meaningful for the creature in whose brain they reside. I conclude by situating my proposal in the context of Harnad's (1990) candidate solution to the symbol grounding problem and responding to three standard objections.

Problems for current causal and teleo-functional theories of content

Causal and teleo-functional attempts to naturalise content are problematic in two ways. First, they take cases of direct sensory contact as basic and offer only promissory notes about how to augment the account to include abstract content. Second, they fail to explain how anything is meaningful for creatures. To elaborate, a direct sensory contact view is worrisome for two reasons. One worry, as Akins (1996) points out, is its reliance on a naïve understanding of sensory systems as simple property detectors. Akins argues that thermoreceptors are unlike thermometers in that they do not function as objective temperature detectors; instead they provide us with relational information to help us meet our thermal requirements by preventing us from getting too hot or too cold to the extent that that is possible. Akins makes the case that sensory systems have to be understood in terms of what they are doing for creatures, which is often not detecting objective properties and so cannot explain the content of a mental representation of that objective property. Indeed, there are many cases in which sensory systems do not provide accurate representations and their evolutionary value is in not doing so (Viger, 2006a).[5]

A second difficulty for accounts of mental content based on direct sensory contact is that they fail to generalise to abstract content. But as we have just seen, a main reason for endorsing RTM is to explain abstract content. If something is present we can respond to it directly, without requiring a mediating representation. And if a representation isn't activated in direct sensation, direct sensing can't explain how a representation gets its content. It is when something is not or cannot be present that we require a representation for it, such as when we engage in abstract planning. This suggests that a different starting point is worth exploring, one that can handle any kind of content. I am not denying that sensation has an important role in explaining mental content: Our way of sensing the world almost certainly influences our way of representing it. If we determine what our sensory systems are doing for us, as Akins suggests, we may come to understand what is meaningful for us, as Harnad requires. Indeed, I propose to develop just such an account. What I am challenging is that it is in virtue of sensing something that our mental representations have the content they do.

Presentations and symbols

To develop a theory of mental content by starting with instances of sensing something seems compelling since, for example, my staring at a tree can often explain why my thoughts are about it — why the tree often activates TREE in me.

However, what needs to be explained is why that mental representation has the content *treehood* for me. The reason the causal relation can appear to explain why the symbol has the content it does is because of an equivocation between two notions of mental representation. In the first, our sensory systems transduce information from something so that we can modify our behaviour — as in the case of the tree. I refer to these kinds of mental representations as *presentations*. But presentations are all stimulus-bound, so they are not the mental representations that we use in most of our thinking, which is not stimulus bound. In the abstract cases highlighted by Brentano, a mental representation stands in for something that is not present. I refer to such mental representations as *symbols*.[6] It is the content of symbols that requires explanation. Sensory contact can often explain how something is present to us and why we activate the symbols we do. However, an account of the content of the symbol is still needed, and it must respect the grounding constraint that the symbol is meaningful for the creature in which it is activated.

The dual route model of vision

Based on research using macaque monkeys, and human subjects both with and without brain damage, Milner and Goodale (1995, 1998, 2004) propose that neural pathways from the primary visual cortex separate into two distinct and largely encapsulated streams, one dorsal and one ventral. "[I]t seems likely that the visual projections from primary visual cortex to the temporal and parietal lobes in the human brain may involve a separation into ventral and dorsal streams similar to that seen in the monkey" (Milner & Goodale, 1998, p. 2).

People with brain damage to the dorsal stream suffer from optic ataxia, a visuomotor disorder that makes it difficult to reach for and grasp objects. These people, surprisingly, can accurately report the location and orientation of the objects they fail to grasp. People with ventral stream damage suffer from visual form agnosia; they are unable to recognise forms, objects and even orientations. Milner and Goodale conclude that the dorsal stream guides real-time action in a dynamic environment, such as reaching, grasping, and ducking, whereas the ventral stream is for object recognition.[7]

The contrast between the streams is quite striking and reflects the distinct purposes of each. For one thing, the dorsal stream is not subject to many of the illusions that we experience via the processing in the ventral stream. For example, in a three-dimensional version of the Ebbinghaus illusion,[8] subjects who see the centre circles as being different sizes, nonetheless adjust their grip in reaching to grasp them in the same way, as if they are the same size (Goodale & Milner, 2004). The dorsal stream must be accurate in guiding behaviour, whereas the ventral stream's role is to "permit the formation of perceptual and cognitive representations which embody the enduring characteristics of objects and their significance" (Milner & Goodale, 1995) to guide more conceptual tasks. The point is to process information in such a way that it can be used by other, nonvisual, systems, such as those involved in generating inferences, planning, memory, and emotions. Visual recognition extends beyond the visual module to thoughts and behaviours in some way related to the visual stimulus. Indeed, successful object recognition often leads to processing in other systems such as recalling previous experiences, or inferring something about the behaviour of what is recognised. So the ventral stream must interface with other systems in precise ways, and it is these interface sites[9] that are the key to grounding symbols on my account.

Forming interfaces

A symbol allows us to think beyond our immediate circumstances by standing in for something that is absent. Thus, a symbol must have the same cognitive effect as the thing would have if it were present. But a visually present stimulus primes an interface site, causing precise activations in many different cognitive systems. And while dual routes of the sort identified for vision have not been demonstrated for other sensory modalities, we do recognise objects using every modality. The smell of freshly baked cookies may bring back memories and the associated happy feelings of childhood; a high-pitched whine may recall the unpleasantness of the dentist's office, etc. So it is plausible that each sensory modality must interface with other cognitive systems in much the way the ventral visual stream does. This implies that the recognition of an object primes an interface site regardless of how it is sensed. Thus, symbol activation must prime the same interface site — the same cognitive systems and in the same way — that what it stands in for does; that's just what it is to function as a stand-in.

What we want to know then, is how something is able to prime the relevant cognitive systems and thereby function as a symbol. Attempting to answer this question highlights just what is at issue in the symbol grounding problem: Is the symbol system people use in thinking innate? The reason this question is important is that the interface sites between different cognitive systems cannot be innate, since the cognitive operations they make accessible, such as retrieving relevant memories or determining appropriate behaviours, emotions, and inferences, are derived from experience.[10] So what's at issue is whether we have a compositionally structured symbol system prior to the formation of the interfaces. My view is that we do not. This is contrary to the accepted view of how RTM fits with CTM, namely Jerry Fodor's language of thought hypothesis (LOT) (Fodor, 1975), so before presenting my account of how symbols are grounded, I mention some difficulties with LOT in regards to the symbol grounding problem.

From my analysis, adopting LOT begins to make the symbol grounding problem look intractable. First, the compositional structure of LOT alone cannot ground the content of its symbols. It was arguing this — following Searle (1980) — that led Harnad (1990) to pose the symbol grounding problem in the first place. Second, attempts to account for meaning by determining a relation between a symbol and its extension are inadequate because the relation is not one to which infants are sensitive. The point is not just that infants are unable to detect the relations suggested so far in naturalistic theories of content (though there might be such a relation we simply have not found yet). None of the kinds of relations that these theories entail could be relations that infants are able to detect. The reason is that symbols in LOT are presumed to be meaningful to the infant *prior* to her having any experience with the world, so whatever the proposed relation is, it is an uninstantiated relation, hence undetectable.[11] Finally, if we have symbols prior to the interfaces, which are required for object recognition, our conceptual capacity outstrips our recognitional capacity. Fodor (1998b) endorses this position at the expense of solving the symbol grounding problem. Fodor (1975) argues that to learn a predicate in a natural language, we must already be able to use a coextensive predicate, which means that we reliably, truly predicate the property it expresses about things. One way to do so would be by recognising them, but since that is precluded, the predication is a purely syntactic process that is ungrounded.[12]

Given the shortcomings of LOT, my approach is to take the formation of interfaces between cognitive systems as prior to the acquisition of symbols. My view is that the symbol system is acquired and that process is what grounds it. To begin, it is important to realize that the interfaces are not simply connections made between pre-existing cognitive operations. The operations themselves are formed through experience, as is evident in the case of what memories can be retrieved. But even in less obvious cases, such as what behaviours a stimulus will prime, the baby's experience greatly augments any innate behavioural dispositions she may already possess. Her experiences of how she can behave, which include her ability to recognise affordances the stimulus presents, how she has interacted with it in the past, what she has seen others do with such things, and what she has been taught to do with it all contribute to what behaviours may be primed for activation (cf. MacDorman, 1999). It is important to notice the role that socialisation plays in developing a culturally-appropriate set of behaviours. In one culture certain insects will tend to produce gathering and eating behaviours while in another

culture they will tend to produce swatting behaviour. The influence of socialisation on inferential dispositions is even more obvious since we are often explicitly
taught reasoning techniques and the conclusions that we are likely to draw depend
on our culturally-embedded interests. So experience — including enculturation
— influences the formation of an interface in determining both what cognitive
operations are present to be interfaced and which ones do interface.

It is also important to stress that the syntactic processing in LOT has no role
for affective states except that they can hinder the performance of the system,
which is another serious shortcoming in trying to ground symbols. According to
my alternative, the production of appropriate affective states is among the cognitive operations that interface, so that part of what object recognition consists in is
the production of an appropriate emotion for that object. This might be realized
by projections that exist between the prefrontal cortex, which is involved in object
recognition, and the amygdala, which is involved in producing our affective states
(Newman & Grace, 1999). What we take something to be is inextricably linked
to how it matters to us, a key aspect of symbol grounding. And as in the case of
behaviour, how something matters to us can be innate or derived from experience.
For example, some emotional responses, such as a strong fear reaction to sudden
loud noises, might be innate, others might be socially determined, such as rever-
ence for a religious artefact.

Because interface sites are formed through experience, their structure changes
over time. As we become more familiar with something, we develop new ways to
interact with it. We learn things about it that influence how we think about it. How
it affects us emotionally can change, and we acquire new memories. That the structure of interfaces is dynamic is expected because we recognise things in the context of our changing experience, and it is in priming activation in other cognitive
systems via these precise interfaces that we come to recognise them. How precise
the interfaces are determines the extent to which we can recognise something, and
they clearly must be precise enough to enable us to discriminate stimuli according
to our conceptual categories. But as long as the interface remains precise enough
for discrimination, the exact structure can be dynamic.[13] Moreover, once an interface is precise enough to discriminate stimuli according to some conceptual
category, we can acquire a symbol for that category.

Grounding symbols

Among the behaviour human infants learn from their social environment is verbal
behaviour.[14] They pick up the verbal patterns in their environment and learn to

produce them; they learn to name the objects they sense. In so doing an interface is created between sensory systems and word production, making the ability to produce words in response to stimuli an aspect of object recognition for the baby. Learning words is one means by which a baby can learn to discriminate categories. But the ability to produce words in response to stimuli does not make them symbols for the baby — though the mother often interprets them and such, as Cowley argues (2007) — because they do not stand in for the stimulus. As I argued above, a symbol must prime the same interface site that what it stands in for does. Now that we understand something of the dynamic structure of such interfaces, we can explain how symbols prime activation in those sites.

A symbol, like a natural language word or an icon,[15] is itself an environmental stimulus, that is, a physical pattern such as an event, including actions and the verbal production of words, or an object, which we sense and recognise. As such, our sensory processing of a symbol, typically visual, auditory or tactile, can be presentational or symbolic.[16] The processing of a symbol such as a verbally produced word is presentational when we respond to the word as a noise (i.e., without recognition), as when a sudden loud voice startles us. To recognise a word, the auditory processing must interface with other cognitive systems, as occurs for anything else we recognise. But for words, I claim there are two special interfaces: one grounds syntax, the other semantics. One interface is with the language faculty in virtue of which a word has the formal syntactic properties it does within a natural language. This interface is tangential to my purposes in this paper.[17] The other interface I am positing is what makes the discriminated environmental pattern a symbol, according to my view. My thesis is that a symbol is neurally encoded with a projection to the interface site of what the symbol stands for, and that this projection, rather than some causal connection to its extension, determines the content of the symbol. When the symbol is activated, the projection primes further activation in the very cognitive systems primed by the thing it stands for. The projection creates a new pathway to that interface site, and, as a result, creates a way of activating cognitive operations without the presence of the stimulus that normally activates those operations — normally meaning in the context of object recognition. The cognitive power of a symbol is the new access it gives us to our mental states, access that is not stimulus bound.

For the acquisition of at least our first symbols, our first words, the projection is likely made possible by the symbol stimulus and what it stands for being present simultaneously, which may explain the intuition underpinning so many naturalistic theories of meaning that propose direct sensation grounds content. The error is to suppose that content is constituted by a causal relation between the symbol and its extension, an account which cannot generalise to abstract contents.

Content arises from the projection in virtue of which the symbol functions as a stand-in, and because the cognitive operations to which it projects are affect-laden and enculturated, the content is grounded. While co-occurrence of a symbol and something in its extension may facilitate creation of a projection, it is the creation of the projection and not direct sensory contact that is basic to a naturalistic theory of content. As a result, accounting for the content of an abstract symbol is not theoretically different from accounting for that of concrete objects. In both cases an interface is created and a word projects to that interface. The only difference is that in the abstract case direct experience can never play a role in forming the interface, though it often doesn't in concrete cases either. My acquisition of "shark" was more like my acquisition of "unicorn" than that of "tree".[18]

Where experience does not mediate the formation of an interface, it is likely that some language is required to do so. To learn "unicorn" a child is shown drawings of unicorns, told stories about them that she remembers and can repeat,[19] etc., from which she is prepared to draw inferences about them, may come to have feelings for them, and would even visually recognise one were she to see it. It is to these operations that the neural encoding of the word "unicorn" projects.[20]

My account so far offers an explanation for how symbols come to have the content they do and why that content matters to us. There are still two aspects of symbol grounding I need to discuss. The first is that social norms constrain the use of symbols. The culture we live in determines what symbols mean to us and how we use them. The physical stimulus that serves as a symbol token is conventional and if we do not conform to the conventions of our society we misuse it. Adults correct children's word production if it does not conform to the historically rooted customs of use that they themselves have learned. In the context of my proposed architecture, learning societal norms amounts to getting the right systems interfaced, so our intersubjective relations influence the very structure of our cognitive system.

The second issue of grounding concerns consciousness and understanding. An appropriately grounded symbol system is one that is meaningful to the creature that has it. That our symbols access our experiences and feelings is a first step, but we can be consciously aware of what our symbols mean and, at least in the case of humans, it is this stronger sense of meaning that must be explained. Now it is well beyond the scope of this paper to defend an account of consciousness from which our phenomenology can be derived, but I will sketch how this might be developed. Many theories of consciousness, such as those proposed by Dennett (1991), Rosenthal (2005), Carruthers (1996, 2000), and Brook and Raymont (forthcoming), accept that higher order representations or dispositions either are, or give rise to consciousness. Higher order representations are a kind of self-monitoring, which, if directed toward the activation of a symbol, would make us conscious of what the symbol had primed.[21] We would be aware that appropriate memories, inferences, feelings and behaviours could be activated, which just might be the feeling of understanding.[22] When we monitor our activated symbols they are meaningful for us.

Symbol systems

Harnad posed the symbol grounding problem for entire symbol systems. "How can the semantic interpretation of a formal symbol system be made intrinsic to the system, rather than just parasitic on the meanings in our heads?" The reason for taking an entire symbol system as the starting point is that human thought as reflected in our speech has systematic regularities, namely productivity and systematicity (Fodor & Pylyshyn, 1988). Thought is productive in that we can think an unbounded number of thoughts, and it is systematic in that the ability to think certain thoughts entails the ability to think certain other thoughts; for example, a mind that can think the thought expressed by "Phil pushes Adam" can also think that "Adam pushes Phil." The explanation for the productivity and systematicity of thought is that there is a representational medium of thinking which is compositional: A finite number of primitive representations can be combined according to recursive rules. Productivity follows from recursion, and systematicity is a result of the fact that parts and a rule for combining them admit interchangeability. Since the rules are syntactic, the system has formal properties and, hence, a formal symbol system that is the medium of thinking. Thus, it is formal symbol systems that need grounding. Moreover, since compositionality is a defining characteristic of a language, this reasoning leads to the conclusion that we have a language of thought (LOT).

One of the central tenets of LOT is that complex representations have constituent structure. The symbol "Jasmine" is a physical component of "Jasmine likes ice cream." Thus, it is supposed that the computations constituting thinking are the physical manipulations of these constituent symbols, a view that has become known as the classical computational theory of mind. Antirepresentationalist alternatives to LOT, most notably connectionism, dynamical systems, and subsumption architecture, were developed in light of significant difficulties that arose from using the classical approach in AI research, such as the frame problem.[23] Though there are things these alternative systems do very well, they are inadequate in the cases raised by Brentano's problem, which was a main reason for accepting RTM in the first place. Even proponents of these views accept that we cannot completely dispense with representations.[24] Thus, RTM is widely accepted — for example, connectionist systems are taken to have distributed representations — and the debate is about finding the right computational model for the mind. The main challenge to connectionism as an alternative to LOT is that its distributed representations either have constituent structure or they do not. If they do, connectionism is not an alternative to LOT. Rather, it is an implementation of it. If not, connectionism is empirically inadequate as a model of thought since it cannot explain compositionality (Fodor & Pylyshyn, 1988).[25]

It is in the context of this debate about cognitive architecture that Harnad posed the symbol grounding problem. A formal symbol system on its own is not enough to explain cognition; it must be grounded. Alternatively, the classical approach leads to problems such as the frame problem because the symbol system does not provide understanding. What Harnad puts forward as a solution to the symbol grounding problem is a move within the representationalist-connectionist debate. He proposes a hybrid model in which classical symbols are grounded in what he refers to as nonsymbolic iconic and categorical representations. Symbols, specifically names for object and event categories, are assigned to categorical representations, which are detectors for invariant features of the object and event categories named. Harnad suggests a connectionist model as the mechanism for learning the invariant features (Harnad, 1990). Thus, Harnad opts for the first horn of Fodor's and Pylyshyn's dilemma in which connectionism is a way of implementing a formal symbol system; however, Harnad's emphasis on symbol grounding gives connectionism a prominent role in the overall cognitive architecture.

Situating my position in this debate, I am also opting for the first horn of the dilemma. Because of my reasoning that the symbols are not innate, *pace* Fodor, I call my view the acquired language of thought hypothesis (ALOT); the symbol system we acquire is a natural language. Though I have focused on symbol grounding, the symbols have syntactic features so they can be structured into complex symbols that express propositions. The interfaces that ground content in ALOT play much the same role that categorical representations do in Harnad's hybrid model, though interfaces have significant non-sensory structure to handle abstract content. The cognitive operations that interface may well be connectionist networks but I take that to be an empirical issue yet to be settled. Harnad sees connectionism as a natural mechanism for learning invariant features of object and event categories; I'm not committed to there being such invariants. Finally, an addition I make to Harnad's proposal is to explore how consciousness is involved in the phenomenology of understanding.

There is one more important sense in which the symbols form a system. The symbols are interconnected to form a network, whereby the activation of any one symbol can in principle activate any other symbol and hence the operations to which it projects. In this way symbol activation is not stimulus bound and comes under our control in the sense that our self-mediated mental states determine the content of our occurrent thoughts.[26] The interconnected network is like a roadway through the mind, a constructed central superstructure that makes for easier travel among the modular cognitive operations embedded within this superstructure.

Objections and replies

I now formulate three standard objections that Fodor raises against alternatives to LOT as they apply to ALOT.

Objection 1, Part 1. To defend psychological explanation in the face of eliminativism, Fodor and Lepore argue that there must be psychological laws that generalise over contentful states. According to holistic theories of meaning, content changes over time so that no two people or one person at different times have symbols with the same content. Insofar as ALOT posits an interconnected lexical network it seems to be a holistic theory of meaning (Fodor & Lepore, 1992).

Reply to Objection 1, Part 1. I have included the first part of this objection simply to distance myself from holistic theories of meaning. The lexical connections are not constitutive of content, so the worry does not apply to ALOT.

Objection 1, Part 2. Since the interfaces which ground content are dynamic, they are never the same between two people and change over time for individuals. So again the symbols of ALOT do not have the same content, and psychological generalisation is not possible.

Reply to Objection 1, Part 2. The interfaces ground content, but the content of a symbol is the property whose instantiation primes the interface site to which the symbol projects. So the symbol TREE means *treehood* for all of us. What this highlights is that ALOT is an account by which we can have the same concepts in different ways, preserving psychological explanation while respecting cognitive differences across individuals and cultures.

Objection 2. According to ALOT the precondition for acquiring a word is having the relevant interface. To learn a word one must have the concept it expresses (Fodor, 1975), so having an interface gives us a concept. Concepts are the constituents of thoughts so they must compose. But interfaces don't seem to be the sorts of things that do compose, so they can't be concepts.

Reply to Objection 2. I'm a Dennettian about concepts. Since I'm already committed to the view that we can have concepts in different ways, it's a small step to accepting that in at least the vast majority of cases[27] there is nothing necessary or sufficient to having a concept. Having a concept is simply having a cluster of competences and behaviours, namely, those that interface, such that one is judged to have the concept from the intentional stance (Dennett, 1987); having a concept is a matter of degree. However, like all matters of degree there are instances where we are clearly on one side of the line or the other. Having a symbol project to an interface is a special way of having a concept, and when we have concepts in this way, as all language users do, we are able to compose our concepts to form propositional thoughts. What this objection commits me to is that non-human animals capable of compositional thoughts have (limited) symbol use. But I take the arguments against non-human animals having a language to show that these are quite exceptional cases.

Objection 3. According to my formulation of ALOT, I am committed to the thesis that the medium of thinking is a natural language. However, animals and human infants without a natural language think. Furthermore, natural language is ambiguous in ways that thoughts are not. For example, the sentence, "I am a philosopher," is ambiguous until the referent of the indexical "I" is specified. However, the thought I mean to express by uttering the sentence is not ambiguous. In thought, the referent is specified, so however I express the referent to myself, it is not with the English "I." It follows that some other medium is required to express the propositions we entertain (Fodor & Pylyshyn, personal communication).

Reply to Objection 3. First, ALOT is committed only to the view that natural language is the medium of some thinking, namely compositional thinking, so the fact that nonverbal animals and human infants think is not an objection to my view. The processes activated by an interface are cognitive and are presupposed for the acquisition of language, so clearly a natural language is not the medium of those processes.

As for the main point of the objection, it refers to cases like indexical terms such as "this" and "I." But "this," like every other symbol we neurally encode, is grounded, likely in some kind of attentional mechanism such as Pylyshyn's visual indexes (Pylyshyn, 2003), so it is not ambiguous when we activate it in thought. The encoding of the word projects to something like a visual index, which determines the referent. In being grounded, words have meaning for us in addition to their ambiguous meanings as part of the language. The problem itself is an artefact of taking an ungrounded symbol system as the starting point.[28]

Conclusion

I have given an account of symbols, and most notably the words of a public language, as environmental stimuli to which we conventionally assign norms of use. We internalise natural language words, encoding them into neural structures. This process gives us mental symbols. The neural encodings of words have three distinct types of connections. The grounding connections are projections to interface sites that are primed by what the symbols stand in for. It is in virtue of these projections that a symbol can stand in for something else; the projections enable the symbol to activate the same cognitive operations as what it stands in for. Symbols are also interconnected to form a network so that the activation of one symbol can activate another, which means the activation is not stimulus bound but rather determined by our mental states. Finally, the symbols have syntactic features that the language faculty can operate over, giving them a compositional structure from which complex symbols can be formed to express propositions.

The acquired language of thought hypothesis is a representational theory of mind that proposes a cognitive architecture in which symbols can be grounded in much the same vein as Harnad's proposed solution and in many ways ALOT is an elaboration of his view. Even if the proposed structure is basically correct, there is much to be done to solve the symbol grounding problem. We have to determine how interfaces are formed, particularly since many objects have common detectable properties, and how projections to interface sites are created, to say nothing of the role of consciousness. Many of the models in this volume are exploring these very issues.

Notes

I would like to thank the following people who have helped me in developing my ideas: Tim Kenyon, Robert Stainton, and the other participants at the Language and Cognition Workshop in Uruguay (May 2006), members who attended my presentation at the meetings of the Canadian Philosophical Association at York University in Toronto (May 2006), especially my commentator James McGilvray, and the participants at the ESG2006 conference in Plymouth (July 2006), especially the organizers Tony Belpaeme, Stephen Cowley, and Karl MacDorman, and three anonymous referees for helpful feedback on this material. Thanks also to the Social Sciences and Humanities Research Council of Canada and the University of Western Ontario for financial support of my research.

1. Clark has added the unruly, such as all of the blue things I have owned in the last two years, to this list of what he calls 'representation hungry problems' (1997, p.167). For ease of exposition I will refer to all of these as cases of abstract content.

2. I use italics for the content of a representation, capitals for a mental symbol, and quotes for natural language words. So the content of DOG is *the property of being a dog* or *doghood* for short, which we express in English with "dog." By "activation" of a symbol, I mean "tokening" in the philosophical jargon, but for general readership I will stick with activation talk.

3. See for example, Fodor (1990), Millikan (1984), and Dretske (1981).

4. This idea is new in analytic philosophy. It is central in continental philosophy.

5. They make small perceptual differences salient.

6. Brentano (1874/1973) makes a similar distinction, and there is evidence that as early as the fourteenth century William of Ockham respected this difference (Panaccio, 2004). More recently, Grush (1997) uses the distinction. His notion of presentation is slightly more liberal than mine and he uses stand-ins primarily for emulation in planning action, which is more restrictive than my conception of how we use symbols, but the notions are otherwise very similar. I develop my version of this distinction between presentations and symbols in more detail in Viger 2006b.

7. My presentation in the two preceding paragraphs follows that in Viger 2006b.

8. This is the illusion in which two circles of the same size are surrounded by other circles. In one case the circles are much larger, in the other much smaller. We see the circle surrounded by the larger circles as smaller, though it is not.

9. These interface sites are similar to what Damasio (1989) refers to as convergence zones in that their activation re-stimulates quite precise neural activity. Given the length of axons the subsystems that interface need not be in local proximity to each other; i.e., an interface can activate distributed processing throughout the brain.

10. This is not to deny that we have some innate dispositions to respond behaviourally and emotionally but these are much more coarse-grained then the kind of interface that differentiated object recognition requires.

11. Fodor's recent requirement that concepts be triggered through interaction with the environment (Fodor 1998a) doesn't address this worry. The syntactic forms of the symbols and the compositional structure of LOT are still innate, so the inferential role a symbol can have is still determined syntactically. That is, how LOT functions is independent of any interactions with the world, so those interactions do not ground it.

12. Assuming that we innately possess very sparse interfaces that become richer with experience (see note 10) won't give us recognitional capacities that match the innate conceptual resources we are supposed to have according to LOT. Sparse interfaces do not individuate content finely enough to account for the symbols the infant is supposed to have. For example, infants likely have a withdrawal and fear reaction to large animals, but very little else in terms of innate behaviours. This won't differentiate a bear from lion, yet BEAR and LION are supposed to be innate according to LOT.

13. I return to this issue in Objection 1 below. See also notes 10 and 12.

14. This in no way denies Chomsky's thesis based on the poverty of stimulus argument (Chomsky, 1985) that very much of what's needed to learn a language is innate. The point is simply that "dog" and "chien" are not innate.

15. I take it that many things can function as symbols for us, but for ease of exposition and because they are the symbols that are part of a symbol system, I restrict my discussion to words of natural languages.

16. Note that the distinction between presentations and symbols does not correspond exactly to dorsal and ventral stream processing that leads to action or recognition, as both processes can be used in imaging and both can be stimulus driven.

17. I think the compositionality of thought requires that the medium of thought has syntactic features, so I mention the interface, but it is beyond the scope of this paper to argue for that claim.

18. Thanks to Glenn Parsons for this example.

19. Note that in language mediated cases for instantiated concepts, like SHARK, the stories need not be true. Enculturation is one way in which we can come to have false beliefs.

20. The unicorn example shows that language mediation is a means of forming our own concepts. The difference between UNICORN and SHARK is that empirical findings can cause us to change our understanding of SHARK. Fodor (1998a) characterizes this as the difference between mind-dependent and natural kind concepts. Only things falling in the extension of the latter are suitable for scientific investigation.

21. This might also be what allows us to recognise a word as a word, since it primes its syntactic and semantic projections.

22. Note the similarity to Wittgenstein's discussion of rule following and how to carry on (Wittgenstein 1953).

23. For an overview of the frame problem see Viger, 2006c.

24. Clark refers to Brentano's cases as a class of representation hungry problems (Clark 1997, 166–170). Van Gelder admits that "[t]o be sure, cognition can, in sophisticated cases, involve representation and sequential processing" (van Gelder 1996, 439); Dennett sees words as building blocks for thought processes that aren't possible without words (Dennett 1996, 1998). To my knowledge Brooks is still a holdout (Brooks, 1991).

25. For an excellent overview of this debate see the introduction in Macdonald and Macdonald (1995). The volume contains many of the seminal papers in the debate.

26. MacDorman refers to controlled symbol production as decontextualization, which he takes to be the key feature of a symbol (personal communication). I agree in that while symbols can act as stand-ins once they project to an interface on my view, it is only by being networked that they are not stimulus bound, so networking is essential for us to *use* symbols as stand-ins. Interconnectedness is also essential in Deacon's (1997) and MacDorman's (1999) accounts.

27. If an analytic/synthetic distinction can be made this won't hold for analytic concepts.

28. In Viger 2005 I argue that the logical/formal terms of a natural language need not be in LOT, even if Fodor is correct about predicates, in which case the medium for thoughts involving those terms would have to be a natural language. Given the classical view of CTM, that's most of our thoughts.

References

Akins, K. (1996). Of sensory systems and the "aboutness" of mental states. *The Journal of Philosophy, 93*(7), 337–72.

Brentano, F. (1874/1973). *Psychology from an empirical standpoint*. A. Rancurello, D.B. Terrell, & L. McAlister (Trans). London: Routledge.

Brook, A. & Raymont, P. (forthcoming). *A unified theory of consciousness*. Cambridge, MA: MIT Press.

Brooks, R. (1991). Intelligence without representation. *Artificial Intelligence 47,* 139–159.

Carruthers, P. (1996). *Language, thought, and consciousness: An essay in philosophical psychology.* Cambridge, UK: Cambridge University Press.

Carruthers, P. (2000). *Phenomenal consciousness: A naturalistic theory.* Cambridge, UK: Cambridge University Press.

Chomsky, N. (1985). *Knowledge of language: Its nature, origin and use.* Westport, CT: Praeger.

Clark, A. (1997). *Being there: Putting brain, body, and world together again.* Cambridge, MA: Bradford/MIT.

Cowley, S. (2007). How human infants deal with symbol grounding. *Interaction Studies, 8*(1), 83–104.

Damasio, A. (1989). Time-locked multiregional retroactivation: A systems-level proposal for the neural substrates of recall and recognition. *Cognition, 33*(1–2), 25–62.

Deacon, T. (1997). *The symbolic species: The co-evolution of language and the brain.* New York: Norton.

Dennett, D. C. (1987). *The intentional stance.* Cambridge, MA: Bradford/MIT.

Dennett, D. C. (1991). *Consciousness explained.* Boston: Little, Brown and Company.

Dennett, D. C. (1996). *Kinds of minds: Towards an understanding of consciousness.* London: Weidenfeld and Nicolson.

Dennett, D. C. (1998). Reflections on language and mind. In P. Carruthers and J. Boucher (Eds.), *Language and thought: Interdisciplinary themes* (pp. 284–294). Cambridge: University Press.

Dretske, F. (1981). *Knowledge and the flow of information.* Cambridge, MA: MIT Press.

Fodor, J. (1975). *The language of thought.* Cambridge, MA: Harvard University Press.

Fodor, J. (1990). *A theory of content and other essays.* Cambridge, MA: Bradford/MIT.

Fodor, J. (1998a). *Concepts: Where cognitive science went wrong.* Oxford: Oxford University Press.

Fodor, J. (1998b). There are no recognitional concepts — not even RED. In J. Fodor, *In critical condition: Polemical essays on cognitive science and the philosophy of mind* (pp. 35–48). Cambridge, MA: MIT Press.

Fodor, J. & Lepore, E.. (1992). *Holism: A shopper's guide.* Oxford: Blackwell.

Fodor, J. & Pylyshyn, Z. (1988). Connectionism and cognitive architecture: A critical analysis, *Cognition, 28*(1–2), 3–71.

Goodale, M. & Milner, A. D. (2004). *Sight unseen.* Oxford: Oxford University Press.

Grush, R. (1997). The architecture of representation. *Philosophical Psychology 10*(1), 5–23.

Harnad, S. (1990). The symbol grounding problem. *Physica D, 42*(1–3), 335–346.

Macdonald, C. & Macdonald, G. (Eds.). (1995). *Connectionism: Debates on psychological explanation.* Oxford: Blackwell.

MacDorman, K. F. (1999). Grounding symbols through sensorimotor integration. *Journal of the Robotics Society of Japan, 17*(1), 20–24.

Millikan, R. (1984). *Language, thought, and other biological categories: New foundations for realism*. Cambridge, MA: Bradford/MIT.

Milner, A. D. & Goodale, M.. (1995). *The visual brain in action*. Oxford: Oxford University Press.

Milner, A. D. & Goodale, M. A. (1998). Precis of *The visual brain in action*. *Psyche, 4*, 1–12.

Newman, J. & Grace, A. (1999). Binding across time: The selective gating of frontal and hippocampal systems modulating working memory and attentional states. *Consciousness and Cognition, 8*(2), 196–212.

Panaccio, C. (2004). *Ockham on concepts*. Aldershot, UK: Ashgate.

Pylyshyn, Z. (2003). *Seeing and visualizing: It's not what you think*. Cambridge, MA: MIT Press.

Rosenthal, D. (2005). *Consciousness and mind*. Oxford: Clarendon Press.

Searle, J. R. (1980). Minds, brains, and programs. *The Behavioral and Brain Sciences, 3*(3), 417–457.

Van Gelder, T. (1996). Dynamics and cognition. In J. Haugeland (Ed.), *Mind design II* (pp. 421–450). Cambridge, MA: MIT Press.

Viger, C. (2005). Learning to think: A response to the *Language of thought* argument for innateness. *Mind and Language, 20*(3), 313–325.

Viger, C. (2006a). Is the aim of perception to provide accurate representations? A case for the 'no' side. In R. Stainton (Ed.) *Contemporary debates in cognitive science*. Oxford: Blackwell Publishing Ltd., 275–288.

Viger, C. (2006b). Presentations and symbols: What cognition requires of representationalism. *Protosociology* (Compositionality, concepts and representations II: New problems in cognitive science), *22*, 36–57.

Viger, C. (2006c). The frame problem. In K. Brown (Ed.) *Encyclopedia of Language and Linguistics*, 2nd edition, vol. 4. Oxford: Elsevier Ltd., 610–613.

Wittgenstein, L. (1953). *Philosophical investigations*. G. E. M. Anscombe (Trans). New York: Macmillan.

Life after the symbol system metaphor

Karl F. MacDorman
School of Informatics, Indiana University

After reviewing the papers in this special issue, I must conclude that brains are not syntactic engines, but control systems that orient to biological, interindividual, and cultural norms. By themselves, syntactic constraints both underdetermine *and* overdetermine cognitive operations. So, rather than serving as the basis for general cognition, they are just another kind of empirically acquired constraint. In humans, symbols emerge from a particular sensorimotor activity through a process of *contextual broadening* that depends on the coordination of conscious and nonconscious processing. This process provides the representational freedom and stability that constitute the human brain's solution to the frame problem and symbol grounding problem. Symbol formation and grounding is an ongoing process of generalising constraints from particular contexts, selectively enlisting their use, and re-automating them. This process is central to the self-creation of a language-using person with beliefs, agency, and identity.

Keywords: affordance, conduit metaphor, distributed cognition, embodiment, language of thought, the symbol grounding problem

Introduction

Those writing in this special issue concur that "human interaction and thus human symbols cannot… be reduced to the formal units pinpointed by syntactic analysis" (Belpaeme and Cowley, 2007). In spite of this, nobody draws the logical conclusion. We should stop conceptualising symbol grounding in terms of formal symbol systems. Modelling can proceed without treating 'minds' as syntactic engines. Therefore, I believe we need to rethink the *person problem*:[1] How can human bodies — and perhaps robot bodies — construct themselves into persons by attuning to patterns and norms in their social environments? I believe an approach that addresses this question could satisfy the authors' conviction that, to engage us in talk, robots will need to do more than ground their internal symbols in the world.

For 'walking, talking' persons, operations are dynamic (Thelen & Smith, 1994), and what we do is irreducible to the formal and syntactic (Clocksin, 1998). The ability to use (external) language is rooted in the body, with brains acting as control systems. So, how do human beings accomplish this? Broadly speaking, there seems to be some kind of consensus among the authors. Using the physics of speech (Worgan & Damper, 2007), human beings align to regularities that include patterns of use (Vogt & Divina, 2007). This enables the later development of what can be *described* as symbolic reasoning (Clowes, 2007). Initially, at least, we are not 'internalising' symbols but using them as constraints on what we do (Clowes, 2007; Cowley, 2007; Viger, 2007). What we characterise as symbol use (or word use) is the outcome of a culturally-located developmental process.

Researchers in artificial intelligence and robotics have often been reluctant to recognise the magnitude of the task they face. One reason for this is that it is easy to be led astray by the *conduit metaphor* (Reddy, 1979). This metaphor characterises, not the nature of language, but how we talk about it. According to this view, a speaker puts ideas into word-containers that are shunted along a conduit and then taken out by a hearer. Cognitive scientists have elevated this 'putting' and 'taking' with such terms as 'encoding' and 'decoding,' but the basic idea of translating concepts from one head into the local language and then back into someone else's head remains the same.

Given the allure of the conduit metaphor, many have refused to recognise the difference between the problem of grounding *internal* symbols in perceptuo-motor invariances as confronted by formal symbol systems (Harnad, 1990) and the *external symbol grounding problem,* namely, the problem of grounding the *external* symbols and signals of utterance activity. This distinction is crucial, because the evolving cultural resources that shape *human* cognition include these external symbols and signals (Lyon, Nehaniv & Cangelosi, 2007; Vogt & Divina, 2007). External symbol grounding depends on real-time co-action (Cowley, 2007), which includes teaching (Seabra Lopez & Chauhan, 2007), and prompts the rise of perceptual skills (Steels & Belpaeme, 2005). Thus, human beings face not only the challenge common to other species of keeping internal representation grounded in the world but also a quite different challenge of grounding (external) language. Damper and Worgan, Cowley, Clowes, Viger and others are correct in maintaining that, although we begin with the physical properties of utterances, it is only through a developmental process that human beings are gradually induced to discover the power of their formal properties.

Although we talk about language as if it were a conduit, this metaphor blinds us to how agents can use representations in turning themselves into people. This developmental process occurs as representations gradually acquire symbolic properties. When symbolic ways of acting are consistent with an agent's developmental history, they give rise to representations that can stand for objects, including objects that are out of view (Viger, 2007). The ability for symbols to act as stand-ins beyond the context of their initial use is typically viewed as *decontextualisation*. This, however, is to substitute a logical for a developmental point of view. From the perspective of grounding, what happens is more appropriately seen as *contextual broadening*. Thus, to solve the *person problem*, we can simulate how simple causal regularities give rise to contingencies that enable systems to reconfigure embodied representations, including those that depend on the movement of other bodies (Cowley, 2007). This involves simulating the interplay of conscious and nonconscious processing,[2] which has been scandalously ignored by past approaches to symbol grounding (MacDorman, 1999). So, in robotics and artificial intelligence, we have to move from forms of representation that can only be reconfigured by human programmers to forms that have sufficient representational freedom and stability to reconfigure themselves based on the interplay of conscious and nonconscious processing. Nothing else will give an agent symbols it can use with sensitivity to norms to constrain the doings of both its own body and those of other agents (Cowley & MacDorman, 2006). This will provide it with the robust grounding that is required to solve the person problem.

Persons are not formal symbol systems

Just as vacuum tubes and other technologies eventually reach an end of life, so do ideas. Symbol systems as defined in Harnad (1990a) seem to have reached just such an end, because, by definition, they can only operate according to *syntactic* constraints. If other constraints (e.g., perceptual, ecological, biomechanical, epigenetic, evolutionary) are to influence a symbol system, it will be solely by virtue of how they connect its symbols to the objects, events and relations they represent.[3]

However, *if* persons (or their brains) were symbol systems, their cognition would operate according to constraints that were simultaneously biological, interindividual, and cultural (Clocksin, 2004). In short, they would *not* be purely syntactic. *Our brains are not syntactic engines but world-oriented control systems* and, as Vygotsky (1986) saw, follow different *lines* of development in dealing with physical and cultural/intentional entities. It is quite possible that verbal thought and meaning become systematic, generative, and inferentially coherent as a consequence of self-organising brains aligning us as persons to cultural norms (MacDorman & Cowley, 2006). These regularities serve as standards against which we evaluate each other's behaviour from our own perspective and, by doing so, give that behaviour value and meaning (Christensen & Bickhard, 2002; Cowley & MacDorman, 2006). These capacities develop in the affectively rich relationships of infants and their caregivers (Cowley, 2007). Thus, the rule-like regularities of human cognition do not reveal syntax as the underlying, built-in mechanism that governs symbolic reasoning.[4] Rather, these regularities emerge from causal processes that depend on a language-saturated cultural ecology. We exploit both the physical world and sets of categories that are derived from the history of particular cultural domains. As Dennett (1987, 1989) and Ross (2006) argue, we gradually come to use the narrative devices that turn our human bodies into persons.

Fodor (1980) and others have proposed that a syntactically-driven symbol system has *a priori* feature detectors for every natural kind of thing. These detectors set processing in motion and, thereby, instantiate the symbols of the symbol system. An example of this from artificial intelligence is the robot Shakey (Nilsson, 1984). From the standpoint of evolution or neurobiology, however, *a priori* feature detectors do not seem plausible (MacDorman, 1998), as even Fodor admits (Guttenplan, 1994). Those who would fix Good Old Fashioned Artificial Intelligence (GOFAI) misunderstand Harnad (1990a), if they believe the matter of symbol grounding only concerns whether a robot is hardwired with feature detectors or learns them on the fly. Consequently, some have simply proposed to connect a pre-existing symbol system to the world by means of a perceptual learning mechanism, such as a neural network.[5]

This setup spares the old *syntactically-governed* symbol system idea, while appearing to address its grounding. But it misses the force of Harnad's point — that, just as a diagram may guide someone in performing formal geometry, the iconic shape of a symbol's referent must constrain the system in *manipulating* the symbol. Thus, Harnad argues that, *to ground symbols, empirical constraints must augment syntactic constraints.* It is not enough that the pattern recognition mechanism by which symbols are instantiated be learned. Constraints on the rules or rule-like regularities by which symbols are manipulated must also be learned. The reason for this, I would argue, is because ecological relations and experience (and, in human beings, norms and language) influence not only how we recognise what is around us, but also how we reason about it (Wason, 1981; MacDorman, 1999). Fodor (1987, 2000) opts for a similar approach in his solution to the philosopher's version of the frame problem: Empirical constraints need to augment syntactic constraints to eliminate "kooky concepts" and thereby help the system avoid reasoning about things that cannot happen or things that do not change.[6]

Both Fodor and Harnad assume that the main problem with syntactic constraints is that they underdetermine mental representations. In other words, syntactic constraints define too broad a universe of possible mental representations, so that an individual's actual mind is an empirically-delimited subset of that universe. This makes Harnad the 'Gorbachev' of cognitivism: He tries to save the approach while fatally undermining it. He considers formal symbol systems to be something that can be fixed by supplementing syntactic constraints with empirical ones. It is as if, like Fodor, he thinks symbol systems are the only way of making behaviour systematic, generative, and inferentially coherent. This view, however, is mistaken. The *a priori* syntactic constraints of symbol systems not only underdetermine mental representations *but, just as importantly, overdetermine them* by excluding nonsyntactic mental operations. In human beings, syntactic constraints may themselves be a product of cultural evolution (Vogt & Divina, 2007). Moreover, rather than apply the formal symbol system model to the whole of general cognition, one may posit that other kinds of systems supply the richness and parsimony required to represent what the brain needs to manage action. We cannot simply assume symbol systems are the building blocks with which body and brain construct a person. On the contrary, these patterns are likely to exist in the world. Thinking may appear systematic, generative and inferentially coherent, because we use social practices to abstract these patterns from the experience of living in a culture. They get the job done and are socially sanctioned. The historically recent development of writing systems, formal education, and computers have further reinforced the dubious belief that meaning derives mainly from the compositionality of symbols (Luria, 1976).

So, if mental operations are neither formal nor syntactic, the issue of symbol grounding should concern how human bodies construct themselves into walking, talking persons from their social environments. It should concern not just the learning of perceptual invariants but also the simulation of persons who can follow (or break) norms and rules. Thus, we are interested in how agents can be educated to think in ever more (or less) logical ways and how they can develop stories to 'explain' why they do what they do, taking an intentional stance toward themselves and their actions (Dennett, 1987, 1989; Ross, 2006). Through this narrative process, people spin explanatory 'myths.' Indeed, in recent decades people have convinced themselves that cognition is driven by processes that are like a telephone exchange, or a computer, or whatever happened to be the dominant metaphor of the day (Clocksin, 1995).

The conduit metaphor obscures language and cognition

The conduit metaphor (Reddy, 1979) tempts us to compare perception with communication. In both cases, we assume, the world provides information that we decode: For perception, this decoding is dependent on sensory transduction, perceptual inferencing, and modelling (Ullman, 1980). For communication, it depends on using an inner system (a language faculty) to decode a signal in terms of invariants that have determinate value (Jackendoff, 2002; see Port & Leary, 2005, for an opposing view). But the metaphor of carrying information distorts our view of how language is learned, how it functions interpersonally, and how it shapes social cognition. There has been an opinion in some branches of mainstream cognitive science that essentially goes like this:

1. Human beings think in a formal language of thought (LOT), which constitutes the symbolic representations of a symbol system (Fodor, 1975).
2. Operations in LOT depend only on internal syntactic constraints.
3. Nevertheless, LOT maintains semantic correspondences with the external world: When you feed true statements into a LOT-manipulating symbol system, the system produces conclusions that by and large are also true.
4. Since the symbol system operates according to internal syntactic constraints, elementary symbols are innate, given beforehand.[7]
5. Complex representations are composed from an 'alphabet' of these symbols.

According to this viewpoint, communication entails encoding in natural language (e.g., an utterance or email) mental concepts, which are taken to be symbolic representations, and sending them across a conduit (e.g., airwaves or the Internet) to a recipient who then decodes them.[8]

The conduit metaphor comes up short for a number of reasons:

1. For us to communicate, your concepts do not need to divide up the world in exactly the same way as my concepts (Reddy, 1979; Steels & Belpaeme, 2005).
2. There is much more to communication than the transfer of facts about the world expressed as propositions.
   a. Kravchenko (2003, 2006), following Maturana (1976) and Maturana and Varela (1980), argues that human communication — like that of any other animal — must be connotational.
   b. As Cowley and MacDorman (1995) have shown, the descriptive content of an utterance often says little about what is happening between individuals in a relationship and what the utterance means for them. An understanding of prosodic, facial and gestural features of communication as well as context is needed.
   c. As Karl Grammer, Alex Pentland, and others point out (e.g., Grammer, Fieder & Filova, 1997; Pentland, 2005), communication can be conceived of in many ways other than in terms of semantics (descriptive meaning) and pragmatics. For example, during human courtship, nonverbal signals

have a probabilistic quality that can give information about receptiveness to a romantic advance without making a firm commitment, thus allowing 'wiggle room' to back out.

3. There is much scepticism about the internalist assumptions of Fodor's LOT, and many researchers follow Dennett (1991), Clark (1997), Hutchins (1995) and others in viewing language as a process of enacting external patterns.[9] While the idea remains underdeveloped, we construct ourselves in the course of experiencing the external social environment (e.g., Dennett, 1987, 1989; Ross, 2006).

The physical symbol systems hypothesis and its problems are symptomatic of people's belief in the conduit metaphor (Newell, 1980).

Given that symbol systems function according to internal syntactic constraints, how do we ground their symbols in the external world? I have argued for more than 12 years that the whole idea of a system operating according to internal *a priori* syntactic constraints is wrong. Rather, the system's rule-like operation and all its symbols must be learned from the bottom up. They must emerge from and be grounded in sensory projections, motor actions, and affective consequences. The system's operation turns on empirical constraints of which formal syntactic constraints are no more than a subset.

In the early 1990s, I was approaching the symbol grounding problem from Stevan Harnad's viewpoint. Cowley (1994, 1997) was concerned about something else: how features of utterances operate between individuals to closely coordinate their activity and regulate their emotion in real-time. These features can be interpreted in many different ways and, based on his acoustic data from conversations, Cowley saw no reason to privilege text-based 'symbolic' interpretations over those that arise from our acute sensitivity to closely-timed prosodic events (e.g., pitch, rhythm, loudness, voice quality). Cowley was (and remains) very concerned about how language gets bootstrapped by the mother-infant dyad. For example, when a baby reaches for a stuffed dog and makes a vocalisation, the mother often over-interprets this as asking for the dog by pointing at it, and the baby cognitively grows into this over-interpretation through the mother's coaxing (see Tomasello, 2003).

So the question Cowley was asking is: How is it that an utterance that starts off with no meaning comes to serve various functions within the mother-infant relationship and eventually acquires semantic meaning? It may, for example, come to act as a stand-in for an object that is not present (Viger, 2007). Because the features of the utterances, including its symbolic/representational features, are in the environment, I suggested to Stephen Cowley, "That's not the *internal* symbol grounding problem, but the *external* symbol grounding problem." By that I meant, "That's not the problem of how you ground the internal symbols in your head in the external objects, relations and states-of-affairs they represent (as formulated by Harnad, 1990a). Rather, that is the problem of how external utterances and features of utterances (including, but not limited to, symbolic features) can come to regulate affect and coordinate activity between persons (e.g., mother and infant) and eventually stand in for things not present." It is this idea that underlies Cowley's attempts to understand how human infants deal with symbol grounding (Cowley, 2006, 2007; Cowley et al. 2004).

So we have three problems: (1) the problem of grounding internal symbols in external states-of-affairs; (2) the problem of grounding utterances (including prosody and the actual words spoken) and facial, gestural and eye movements in interindividual activity (including affect); and (3) the problem of using robots to investigate not only the first symbol grounding problem but also the extended version having to do with human language.[10]

How brains ground symbols

Being part of a symbol system, Viger (2007) argues, is not the defining characteristic of a symbol but rather its potential to stand in for something that is out of view. But a symbol's potential to function in *different contexts* is equally important, because this is how an agent shows it understands a symbol *as a symbol* and not just as a pattern. This potential is often called *decontextualisation*. While Viger (2007) acknowledges its importance, he notes that it presupposes that the symbol comes first. However, because symbols presuppose an interface, it is more appropriate to posit that the grounding comes first and that the symbol instead emerges from a process of *contextual broadening*. When a baby reaches for a plate and says, "mo," and the mother interprets this to mean, "I would like to have some *more* food," this does not mean "mo" functions as a symbol for the baby. The baby may just be repeating the mother's vocalisation (or its own). It may learn that in this context, vocalising "mo" is a way of acting that gets the mother to approach with food. Only when the baby exhibits an understanding of how "mo" (or "more") functions in different contexts can we say that it knows the vocalisation stands for a particular abstract relation (e.g., between how much it has and how much it wants). In this sense, the baby demonstrates a grasp of the word's meaning through use (Wittgenstein, 1953).

Conscious processing may be implicated in contextual broadening, because persons can think about objects in focal consciousness in ways that indicate the loosening of the objects from context. For example, I can think about binding papers with a stapler or using it to put up posters, but I can also think about the effects of microwaving it, or things I cannot do with it, like throwing it into the sun. This indicates a degree of *representational freedom* for objects in consciousness that might *not* be obtained by strictly nonconscious processing.

But nonconscious processing has its advantages too. It supports the parallel execution of well-honed skills. The reason a FIFA professional can play soccer is because he *doesn't need to think* about how to run or dribble or make a shot. While these things are coming together automatically, he can focus on strategy. If you were to make him think about, for example, ways to improve his shooting, presumably his game would worsen before it improved (Langer & Imber, 1979). Like soccer, learning to drive takes conscious study and effort, but eventually people not only manage to drive but to do many other things while driving. Yet, if something happened on the road, extraneous activities would be interrupted as orienting reactions redirected conscious attention to the unexpected event.

It is precisely because conscious processing is so useful in evaluating novel stimuli that it must be supplemented by other mechanisms. It typically has widespread effects on attention, memory, and motor control (Baars, 1988). While contradictory beliefs may coexist in the subconscious, objects in consciousness are required to maintain a much higher degree of consistency. For example, a locked gate forced me to park my bicycle in a new place, but later without thinking I returned to its usual spot only to find it missing. Outside of consciousness, my brain was quite content to represent the bicycle as residing at its usual location and at its new location. Flexibly maintaining consistent representations in consciousness may be computationally demanding, involving billions of bits of information in the brain being simultaneously and coherently interrelated (MacDorman, 1999, 2004). This may explain why the brain's massively parallel nonconscious processing can break down into serial processing in consciousness (Mangan, 2001). This is not to deny the capacity of nonconscious processing to maintain complex interrelations that have already been worked out through practice. But it is this "working out" that is the domain of conscious processing, because what is represented consciously is articulated with sufficient richness to allow persons to evaluate novel situations.

If solving the *frame problem* entails finding a representational form that allows computational agents to avoid getting bogged down reasoning about stable aspects of the world (Janlert, 1996), the interplay between conscious and nonconscious processing has endowed the human organism with a solution. The brain tolerates inconsistencies until something goes wrong — something unexpected happens. It then sets conscious processing on to the problem — with its flexibility, consistency checks, and integration of disparate brain centres — to correct and reautomate the subconscious routines that led to the error. The result of this process is that human brains can deploy (1) a flexible and consistent representation of objects in consciousness, (2) a vast number of stable subconscious routines that are able to run in parallel, and (3) methods for consciously detecting when things go wrong and correcting and reautomating those routines. Isn't this what an intelligent robot needs to be able to do?

Let us now consider the two major robotics approaches to intelligent behaviour. There is the GOFAI approach of programming a robot to make plans by means of a symbol system and the behaviour-based approach of building up complex behaviours from simple mechanisms that directly link sensing with motor response. The GOFAI approach, which suffers from the usual symbol grounding and frame problems, metaphorically resembles conscious processing, while the behaviour-based approach with its hardwired routines metaphorically resembles some kinds of nonconscious processing. Some researchers have taken a hybrid approach by welding together GOFAI and behaviour-based subsystems along a fixed interface (Malcolm, 1995). But it is clear that none of these approaches attempts to simulate the interplay of conscious and subconscious processing, which is how the human organism has finessed the symbol grounding and frame problems.

Although it is easy to argue that GOFAI-based robots have too much representational freedom, while behaviour-based robots have too little, this argument really misses the point. To illustrate why, it is useful to consider Brooks' robot Herbert (1991a, 1991b). Herbert appeared to perform an intentional activity, collecting soda cans in an office, but it did so without benefit from any form of central symbolic representation. When a sensor detected a can, a switch sent the robot forward. When its collision with the desk stilled the wheels, a gripper extended. When the soda can broke an infrared beam in the gripper, it grasped the can, and so on.

Is Herbert *too grounded* in the situation and therefore lacking representational freedom? I would argue against it, and just because a person can think abstractly about soda cans does not make that person's thinking less grounded than Herbert's responses. Herbert has a brittle kind of grounding, which, oddly, is similar to the GOFAI-based robot Shakey (Nilsson, 1984). Despite their differences, Herbert, like Shakey, is crafted by engineers to perform specific actions on specific items in specific environments (e.g., where desks have a certain height). Neither robot could get very far in a new environment with unknown objects. While well-fitted by a (conscious) designer to a given purpose, neither could reconfigure its internal workings for some new task. Neither robot can discover what objects afford, nor develop and automate skills for handling objects based on their affordances (Gibson, 1979). In other words, they lack the kinds of cognitive systems that, in humans, coordinate conscious and nonconscious processing. Just as traditional symbol systems cannot be grounded without a human interpreter (Harnad, 1990a, 1990b), Brooks' subsumption architecture cannot be grounded without a human designer to rebuild it as the context changes.

Neither Shakey nor Herbert has a mechanism for *re*grounding, which explains why their grounding is so brittle. It fits a certain environment but fails irrecoverably in others. A system with a flexible grounding will reground itself when its body, environment, or even its goals change (MacDorman et al., 2000). Like the babies Cowley (2007) studies, it will be able to use the world to construct its own agency. Unfortunately, however, the apparent grounding of Herbert and Shakey depends on the plasticity of their designers' brains and not their own. And so it is their designers' brains that effectively coordinate processing that is more centralised, articulated, and conscious with processing that is more automated, modularised, and subconscious (MacDorman, 1999). In this manner, information is decontextualised and recontextualised as skills are automated and reautomated. It is these cognitive and sensorimotor processes that make for a robust grounding.

Conclusion

Except in abstract, formal systems, such as those implemented on a computer, even symbolic processing is embodied and situated — and influenced and constrained by its embodiment and other circumstances (Pattee, 2001; Lindblom & Ziemke, 2006). A given body sets up unique ecological relations between its perceptuo-motor and cognitive systems and the environment. Contextual broadening develops from the sensorimotor projections of objects in a *particular* situation. The ability to reason in other, new situations does not involve substituting syntactic constraints for empirically acquired ones but rather acquiring and generalising empirical constraints from a history of interaction and bringing them to bear on the situation at hand. In more abstract planning and reasoning, empirically acquired constraints may take on logic-like properties, but ecological (i.e., body–world) constraints remain at play (Wason, 1981). Even logical constraints are learned empirically. Indeed, logical thinking is just one of many kinds of (learned) habits that afford contextual broadening.

Fodor (1996) has characterised the symbol systems of AI as being subject to the frame problem, because they have too much representational freedom, being governed only by syntactic constraints, while Harnad (1991) has attributed the same cause to the symbol grounding problem. However, I would argue that syntactic constraints are a subset of empirical constraints and not the other way around. Symbol systems do not suffer from too much representational freedom but the wrong kind! In contrast, the human brain effectively manages the trade off between freedom and stability through the interplay of conscious and nonconscious processing, and that is our solution to the frame and symbol grounding problems.

Notes

Much appreciation goes to all the participants in the External Symbol Grounding Workshop in Plymouth, UK on 3 and 4 July 2006, and especially to Tony Belpaeme, Stephen J. Cowley, Stevan Harnad, Alexander Kravchenko, Joanna Raczaszek, and Christopher Viger for fruitful discussions on symbol grounding that have contributed to this paper. I would also like to thank Bruce B. Mangan for a discussion on consciousness and Robert Port for a discussion on spoken language.

1. This label emerged from private correspondence with Stephen J. Cowley.

2. Nowhere in my discussions of consciousness in this paper do I attempt to address the so-called 'hard problem' of why we are even conscious at all. I am merely looking at the *functional* relation between conscious and nonconscious processing — a relation which presumably could be implemented in machines regardless of whether these machines would really be conscious. My treatment of the hard problem appears in MacDorman (2004).

3. They may do so, for example, by virtue of how a mushroom instantiates a *mushroom* symbol in the head and, inseparably, how mushroom-related symbol processing elicits mushroom-directed sensorimotor actions like picking, sorting, washing, frying, and eating.

4. This contrasts with Soar (Laird, Newell, & Rosenbloom, 1987) and other ungrounded reasoning programs implemented on computers.

5. The mechanism performs category induction by learning invariant properties of an object's sensory projections to distinguish the object from confusable alternatives based on internal and external state changes (Harnad, 1987; Cangelosi, Greco & Harnad, 2000).

6. If after the robot has lifted a cup it has to determine whether the French Prime Minister is still in office, it is wasting time reasoning about something that is highly unlikely to have changed. If it has to determine whether Venus has entered its gut, it is wasting time reasoning about something that cannot happen. And if it has to figure out that it should *not* reason about these things, it has already fallen into the frame problem. The solution is to find a representational form that is adequately constrained so that senseless reasoning will not happen.

7. This has been Fodor's assumption. According to Fodor, 1980, these elementary symbols are not something low-level like edges and blobs or other basic perceptual or sensorimotor features, but natural kinds of things: emperor penguins, zebras, and so on.

8. I may have in my head a concept corresponding to the sentence "John saw Mary with her ex-husband." But this concept, as represented in LOT, need not resemble any natural language (It could instead resemble, e.g., Schank and Ableson's Conceptual Dependency, 1977.)

9. This work builds on Vygotsky's (1986) metaphor of *internalising* what begins as external mediational means. While the term *internalising* is much disputed, it can be uses as shorthand for processes like the move from counting on the fingers to counting in the head or from talking to others to thinking in words.

10. Since many animals presumably can consistently perceive relations among objects, and thus enjoy systematicity in their perceptual apparatus (as Fodor and Pylyshyn, 1988, say, "punctate minds don't happen"), I can see the problem of grounding internal symbols as also being an issue for many non-primate species.

References

Baars, B. (1988). *A cognitive theory of consciousness.* Cambridge, UK: Cambridge University Press.

Steels, L. & Belpaeme, T. (2005). Coordinating perceptually grounded categories through language: A case study for colour. *Behavioral and Brain Sciences, 28*(4), 469–489.

Brooks, R. A. (1991a). Intelligence without reason. In *Proceedings of the Twelfth International Conference on Artificial Intelligence (IJCAI),* Sydney, Australia (Vol. 1), pp. 569–595. San Mateo, CA: Morgan Kaufmann.

Brooks, R. A. (1991b). Intelligence without representation. *Artificial Intelligence, 47,* 139–159.

Cangelosi, A., Greco, A. & Harnad, S. (2000). From robotic toil to symbolic theft: Grounding transfer from entry-level to higher-level categories. *Connection Science, 12*(2), 143–162.

Cheney, D. L. & Seyfarth, R. M. (1990). *How monkeys see the world: Inside the mind of another species.* Chicago: University of Chicago Press.

Christensen, W. & Bickhard, M. (2002). The process dynamics of normative function. *Monist, 85*(1), 3–28.

Clark, A. (1997). *Being there: Putting brain, body, and world together again.* Cambridge, MA: MIT Press.

Clocksin, W. (1995) Knowledge representation and myth. In J. Cornwell (Ed.) *Nature's Imagination* (pp. 190–199) Oxford: Oxford University Press.

Clocksin, W. F. (1998). Artificial intelligence and human identity. In J. Cornwell (Ed.), *Consciousness and human identity* (pp. 101–121). Oxford, UK: Oxford University Press.

Clocksin, W. (2004) Memory and emotion in the cognitive architecture. In D. Davis (Ed.) *Visions of Mind* (pp. 122–139) Hershey, PA: IDEA Group.

Clowes, R. (2007). Semiotic symbols and the missing theory of thinking. *Interaction Studies, 8*(1), 105–124.

Cowley, S. J. & MacDorman, K. F. (1995). Simulating conversations: The communion game. *AI & Society, 9*(3), 116–137.

Cowley, S. J. (1994). Conversational functions of rhythmical patterning: A behavioural perspective. *Language and Communication, 14,* 353–376.

Cowley, S. J. (1997). Conversation, co-ordination and vertebrate communication. *Semiotica, 115*(1), 27–52.

Cowley, S. J. & MacDorman, K. F. (2006). What baboons, babies, and Tetris players tell us about interaction: A biosocial view of norm-based social learning. *Connection Science, 18*(4), 363–378.

Cowley, S. J., Moodley, S. & Fiori-Cowley, A. (2004). Grounding signs of culture: Primary intersubjectivity in social semiosis. *Mind, Culture and Activity, 11*(2), 109–132.

Cowley, S. J. (2006). Distributed language: Biomechanics, functions and the origins of talk. In C. Lyon, C. Nehaniv & A. Cangelosi (Eds.), *The Emergence and Evolution of Linguistic Communication* (pp. 105–129). London: Springer.

Cowley, S. J. (2007). How human infants deal with symbol grounding. *Interaction Studies, 8*(1), 83–104.

Dennett, D. C. (1987). *The intentional stance.* Cambridge, MA: MIT Press.

Dennett, D. C. (1989). The origins of selves. *Cogito, 3,* 163–173.

Dennett, D. C. (1991). *Consciousness explained.* Boston: Little, Brown.

Fodor, J. A. (1975). *The language of thought.* New York: Cromwell.

Fodor, J. A. (1980). On the impossibility of acquiring more powerful structures. In M. Piatelli-Palmarini (Ed.), *Language and learning*. London: Routledge.

Fodor, J. A. (1987). Modules, frames, fridgeons, sleeping dogs and the music of the spheres. In Z. W. Pylyshyn (Ed.), *The robot's dilemma: The frame problem in artificial intelligence* (Chapter 8). Norwood, NJ: Ablex.

Fodor, J. A. (2000). *The mind doesn't work that way: The scope and limits of computational psychology.* London: MIT Press.

Fodor, J. A. & Pylyshyn, Z. W. (1988). Connectionism and cognitive architecture: A critical analysis. *Cognition, 28,* 3–71.

Gibson, J. J. (1979). *The ecological approach to visual perception.* Boston, MA: Houghton Mifflin.

Grammer, K., Fieder, M. & Filova, V. (1997). The communication paradox and possible solutions. In A. Schmitt, K. Atzwanger, K. Grammer & K. Schäfer (Eds.), *New Aspects of Human Ethology* (pp. 91–120). New York: Plenum Press.

Guttenplan, S. (1994). Jerry A. Fodor. In Guttenplan, S. (Ed), *A companion to the philosophy of mind.* Oxford, UK: Blackwell.

Harnad, S. (1987). Category induction and representation. In S. Harnad (Ed.), *Categorical perception: The groundwork of cognition.* Cambridge: Cambridge University Press.

Harnad, S. (1990a). The symbol grounding problem. *Physica D, 42,* 335–346.

Harnad, S. (1990b). Lost in the hermeneutic hall of mirrors. *Journal of Experimental and Theoretical Artificial Intelligence, 2,* 321–327.

Hutchins, E. (1995). *Cognition in the wild.* Cambridge, MA: MIT Press.

Jackendoff, R. (2002). Foundations of language: Brain, meaning, grammar, evolution. Oxford: Oxford University Press.

Janlert, L.-E. (1996). The frame problem: Freedom or stability? With pictures we can have both. In K. M. Ford & Z. W. Pylyshyn (Eds.), *The robot's dilemma revisited.* Norwood, NJ: Ablex.

Kravchenko, A. V. (2003). The ontology of signs as linguistic and non-linguistic entities: A cognitive perspective. *Annual Review of Cognitive Linguistics, 1*(1), 179–191.

Kravchenko, A. V. (2006). Cognitive linguistics, biology of cognition and biosemiotics: Bridging the gaps. *Language Sciences, 28*(11), 51–75.

Laird, J., Newell, A. & Rosenbloom, P. (1987). Soar: An architecture for general intelligence. *Artificial Intelligence, 33,* 1–64.

Langer, E. & Imber, L. (1979). When practice makes imperfect: The debilitating effects of overlearning. *Journal of Personality and Social Psychology, 37,* 2014–2025.

Lindblom, J. & Ziemke, T. (2006). The social body in motion: Cognitive development in infants and androids. *Connection Science, 18*(4), 333–346.

Luria, A. R. (1976). *Cognitive development: Its cultural and social foundations.* Cambridge, MA: Harvard University Press.

Lyon, C., Nehaniv, C. L., Cangelosi, A. (2007). Emergence of communication and language. London: Springer.

MacDorman, K. F. (1998). Feature learning, multiresolution analysis, and symbol grounding: A peer commentary on Schyns, Goldstone, and Thibaut's 'The development of features in object concepts.' *Behavioral and Brain Sciences, 21*(1), 32–33.

MacDorman, K. F. (1999). Grounding symbols through sensorimotor integration. *Journal of the Robotics Society of Japan, 17*(1), 20–24.

MacDorman, K. F., Tatani, K., Miyazaki, Y. & Koeda, M. (2000). Proto-symbol emergence. *Proceedings of the IEEE/RSJ International Conference on Intelligent Robots and Systems (IROS),* October 30-November 5, 2000. Kagawa University, Takamatsu, Japan.

MacDorman, K. F. (2004). Extending the medium hypothesis: The Dennett-Mangan controversy and beyond. *Mind and Behavior, 25*(3), 237–257.

MacDorman, K. F. & Cowley, S. J. (2006). Long-term relationships as a benchmark for robot personhood. In *Proceedings of the 15th IEEE International Symposium on Robot and Human Interactive Communication* (RO-MAN). September 6–9, 2006. University of Hertfordshire, Hatfield, UK.

Malcolm, C. M. (1995). The SOMASS system: A hybrid symbolic and behaviour-based system to plan and execute assemblies by robot. In J. Hallam et al. (Eds.), *Hybrid problems, hybrid solutions* (pp. 157–168). Oxford: ISO Press.

Mangan, B. B. (2001). Sensation's ghost: The non-sensory 'fringe' of consciousness. *Psyche, 7*(18).

Maturana, H. R. (1978). Biology of language: The epistemology of reality. In G. Miller & E. Lenneberg (Eds.), *Psychology and Biology of Language and Thought* (pp. 28–62). New York: Academic Press.

Maturana, H. & Varela, F. (1980). *Autopoiesis and cognition: The realization of the living.* Dordrecht, Holland: Reidel.

Newell, A. (1980). Physical symbol systems. *Cognitive Science, 4,* 135–183.

Nilsson, N. J. (1984). Shakey the robot. *Technical Note 323,* SRI AI Center, Menlo Park, CA.

Pattee, H. H. (2001). The physics of symbols: Bridging the epistemic cut. *Biosystems, 60,* 5–21.

Pentland, A. (2005). Socially aware computation and communication. *IEEE Computer, 38*(3), 33–40.

Port, R. & Leary, A. (2005). Against formal phonology. *Language, 81*(4), 927–964.

Reddy, M. J. (1979). The conduit metaphor: A case of frame conflict in our language about language. In A. Ortony (Ed.), *Metaphor and thought.* Cambridge, UK: Cambridge University Press.

Ross, D. (2006). The economics and evolution of selves. *Journal of Cognitive Systems Research, 7,* 246–258.

Schank, R. G. & Ableson, R. P. (1977). *Scripts, goals, plans and understanding.* Hillsdale, NJ: Erlbaum.

Seabra Lopes, L. & Chauhan, A. (2007). How many words can my robot learn? An approach and experiments with one-class learning. *Interaction Studies, 8*(1), 53–81.

Thelen, E. & Smith, L. B. (1994). *A dynamic systems approach to the development of cognition and action.* Cambridge, MA: MIT Press.

Tomasello, M. (2003). *Constructing a language.* Cambridge, MA: Harvard.

Ullman, S. (1980). Against direct perception. *Behavioral and Brain Sciences, 3,* 373–415.

Viger, C. (2007). The acquired language of thought hypothesis: A theory of symbol grounding. *Interaction Studies, 8*(1), 125–142.

Vogt, P. & Divina, F. (2007). Social symbol grounding and language evolution. *Interaction Studies, 8*(1), 31–52.

Worgan, S. F. & Damper, R. I. (2007). Grounding symbols in the physics of speech communication. *Interaction Studies, (8)*1, 7–30.

Vygotsky, L. (1986). *Thought and language.* London: MIT Press.

Wason, P. C. (1981). Understanding the limits of formal thinking. In H. Parret and J. Bouveresse (Eds.), *Meaning and Understanding.* Berlin: Walther de Gruyter.

Wittgenstein, L. (1953). *Philosophical investigations.* Oxford: Blackwell.

Index

In the series *Benjamins Current Topics (BCT)* the following titles have been published thus far or are scheduled for publication: